In 1994 Trevor Dennis joined the [...] he is Vice Dean. For nearly 12 y[...] Old Testament studies at Salisbur[...] During his time at Salisbury, he wrote two books on Old Testament narratives, *Lo and Behold!* (1991), and *Sarah Laughed* (1994), and these were later followed by two volumes exploring Old Testament stories of encounter with God, *Looking God in the Eye* (1998), and *Face to Face with God* (1999). Before going to Salisbury, he was a chaplain at Eton College, and there he began preaching occasionally through storytelling, a practice he has continued ever since. SPCK has published five collections of his pieces, *Speaking of God* (1992), *Imagining God* (1997), *The Three Faces of Christ* (1999), *Keeping God Company* (2002) and *God Treads Softly Here* (2004). In 2003 Lion published his children's Bible, *The Book of Books*. *The Easter Stories* is a companion volume to *The Christmas Stories*, published by SPCK in August 2007, and these two books are his first exploring New Testament narratives in detail. Each of them makes use of the other string to his bow by including a number of his stories and verse meditations. Of the seven pieces in this volume, four have not been published before. He is married to Caroline, and they have four children and two grandchildren.

THE EASTER STORIES

Trevor Dennis

First published in Great Britain in 2008

Society for Promoting Christian Knowledge
36 Causton Street
London SW1P 4ST

British Library Cataloguing-in-Publication Data
A catalogue record for this book is available from the British Library

ISBN 978–0–281–05849–5

1 3 5 7 9 10 8 6 4 2

Typeset by Graphicraft Ltd, Hong Kong
Printed in Great Britain by Ashford Colour Press

Produced on paper from sustainable forests

For Caroline,
for her love,
for her keeping my feet on the ground,
for everything.

Today the curtain is down
The veil drawn over the face,
World only its aspect,
Tree, brick wall, dusty leaves

Of ivy, a bird
Shaken loose from the dust
It is the colour of. Nothing
Means or is.

Yet I saw once
The woven light of which all these are made
Otherwise than this. To have seen
Is to know always.
                    (Kathleen Raine, 'Hidden')

Contents

Contents

Acknowledgements

I would like to thank my colleagues at Chester Cathedral for allowing me to take a three-month sabbatical in the autumn of 2006, and for covering me in my absence. In that time I managed to write this book and its companion volume, *The Christmas Stories*. Without this period of leave I would not have had time to start, let alone complete, either of them.

When we were searching for an appropriate image for the front cover of the book, Andrew Moore, then a student at Chester University and now one of the vergers at the Cathedral, sent me a reproduction of the Velasquez *Supper at Emmaus*. It was precisely what we wanted. Another friend of mine, Christine Bull, sent me the text of Kathleen Raine's poem, 'Hidden', and thereby provided exactly what I was looking for as a preface. I am very grateful to them both for their help.

Jan Dean gave me permission to quote some lines from an unpublished poem, 'Pilgrim Days', which she wrote for the Cathedral's previous Education Officer, Judy Davies, when she retired in October 2006. Jan is a published poet, and I am very grateful to her, both for her permission and her generosity.

'Hidden', by Kathleen Raine, is reprinted by permission of the Estate of Kathleen Raine from *The Presence* (© Kathleen Raine, Golgonooza Press, Ipswich, 1987).

'Alive', by R. S. Thomas, from *Collected Poems 1945–1990*, is reprinted by permission of J. M. Dent, a division of the Orion Publishing Group.

I am most grateful to Alison Barr, Senior Editor at SPCK, for encouraging me to write on the New Testament and for all she has done towards *The Easter Stories*' publication. I would also like to record my thanks to other members of the SPCK team, including Sally Green and Monica Capoferri, and to Trisha Dale, the sharp-eyed and sensitive copy-editor.

Acknowledgements

By far the greatest debt I owe is to my wife Caroline, who has put up with me for a rather long time now. This book is dedicated to her.

1

The torn veil

Thin places, thin moments, thin people

I had wanted to find the place for years. My family and I lived in Salisbury for over 11 years, and during that time we had visited the nearby Stonehenge many a time, preferring to approach the stones on foot from the south along the old grassy drove road. The smaller 'blue stones' there came originally from the Preseli Hills in Pembrokeshire. North Pembrokeshire was a favourite part of the world for us and we had many family holidays there. The coastline is as fine as anywhere in Britain, and in the north the wild Preseli Hills rise immediately behind it. The birds there are wonderful, too. The books about Stonehenge said the blue stones came from a particular spot in the hills called Carn Menyn. I had the Ordnance Survey maps, but I couldn't find Carn Menyn anywhere. Not until 2005, when my wife Caroline and I were staying in a cottage a little further to the east than the ones we had rented in the past. I was poring over the two-and-a-half-inches-to-the-mile map of the area, looking at the local tracks and paths, and there it was, Carn Menyn! I could see why I had missed it before. It is what would be called in Devon a tor, and is in the middle of a group of rocky outcrops on wide moorland, in the shadow of a hill whose summit even at a distance is humped by a series of huge Bronze-Age burial mounds. We could actually see it from where we were staying!

There were few people walking the hills the day Caroline and I set out for Carn Menyn. We passed a thin straggle of a tor, looking for all the world like the spine of a buried Welsh dragon. Ravens called softly as they flew overhead. We found the spot easily enough. There was nobody else to be seen when

1

we got there. I had gone out of curiosity, and because we both love walking those hills. I did not expect to find anything especially unusual. I just wanted to go to the place where they said the blue stones came from. I was surprised. We could see one reason why they had chosen the place for their stones. Great monoliths, already cracked apart and carved by frost and wind, stood vertical or lay scattered around our feet. Yet there was another reason, perhaps. I at once felt we were on holy ground. I had not expected it. I had thought I would be merely interested by the place. I could not help wondering whether four thousand years ago the people who built Stonehenge had felt the same. For me it was what some people call a 'thin place', a place where the veil between heaven and earth is woven lightly and has a certain transparency about it. I had not expected it.

Even more unexpected for me was the Chapel of the Burning Bush in the Church of the Transfiguration at St Catherine's Monastery in the Sinai desert. I was helping to lead a pilgrimage to the Sinai from Chester Cathedral where I work. The sixth-century monastery is in the heart of the peninsula, but a fast tarmac road brings the coaches from the cruise ships moored at Sharm el Sheikh, and since the monastery only opens its doors to most visitors during a few hours in the morning, it gets so crowded you can hardly move. But we had written ahead and got permission to go behind the iconostasis of the church, to see the magnificent sixth-century mosaic of the transfiguration of Christ in the apse of the sanctuary. Beyond that was the Chapel of the Burning Bush. We were not allowed right into the chapel, but having passed through a narrow door had to stop at a gate and peer in. It was very small. I was bringing up the rear, and there was no other party immediately behind us. I did not expect to be moved by the place.

I find myself captivated by the story of the burning bush in the Bible. I have written about it in one of my books, *Face to Face with God*, and it keeps cropping up in my sermons. It is one of the great biblical stories of encounter with God, and is written with a wonderfully light touch. But the writer has taken care to put it off the map. He describes it in Exodus 3.1

as being 'behind the desert'. As Robert Alter has remarked, the phrase is an odd one (*The Five Books of Moses*, 2004, p. 318). He suggests it might mean 'deep into the desert', though he simply has 'into the wilderness' in his translation (not so Everett Fox, who in his own more literal translation of *The Five Books of Moses* (1995, p. 269), has 'behind the wilderness'; the NRSV has 'beyond the wilderness'). I want to preserve the strangeness of the Hebrew expression. In *Face to Face with God* (1999, p. 4), I wrote this: 'Where are we? We are "behind the desert", in the back of beyond. We are in mysterious country, beyond the edges of maps, beyond human knowledge, nearly beyond human imagining. We have entered upon the very mystery of God.'

But I did not expect to enter upon the very mystery of God as I peered into the Chapel of the Burning Bush at St Catherine's Monastery. I am not a great one for trying to fix what cannot be fixed, for trying to pin heaven to earth and say, 'This is the spot where so and so took place.' It is important for some, but not for me. Before we entered the church of the monastery, we passed what guides were insisting was the burning bush itself. To me their claims were ridiculous and made me slightly irritated. They did the story in Exodus no favours. They robbed it of its mystery and its holiness, and reduced it to a not very prepossessing clump of foliage. The Exodus story was *art*, high art, not to be reduced to bathos by any absurd claim that it literally happened, and any solemn assurance, 'Here, ladies and gentlemen, you have the proof: the very bush itself!' So I was not expecting it, when I bent my head through the narrow door and paused at the gate of the Chapel of the Burning Bush, and the holiness of the place caught me by the throat.

There are some places where I expect to find holiness. Chester Cathedral is one of them, though its holiness has crept up on me slowly over the years. Every year we have a week of Pilgrim Days organized by our Education Officer, when the Cathedral gets taken over by junior-school children. In recent years a local poet called Jan Dean has led a poetry workshop, and has coaxed extraordinary poems from the children. When Judy Davies our previous Education Officer retired, Jan wrote a poem for her and recited it at one of her leaving parties. It included these lines:

> Inside this great building
> another secret building rises –
> here a soul can spread into the space,
> breathe and fill and feel a part
> of all the people who have ever stood, or sat,
> or sighed, or sung in this stone place.

I recognize what Jan Dean means.

I know I will always find holiness in Stanley Spencer's chapel at Burghclere, the Sandham Memorial Chapel, as it is called, whose east, north and south walls are entirely covered by his paintings relating to his experiences during the First World War. I look back to the days when I first discovered the place. It was in the care of the National Trust, as it still is, but it was left unattended, and was visited by remarkably few people. It was flanked by a couple of almshouses, and if nobody was already there when I arrived, and usually nobody was, I found a sign in front of the door of the chapel pointing either right or left, depending on who was minding the key that day. I recall a delightful Geordie women in one of the houses, who would hand me the great key and I would go and open the door and at once be confronted by the figures crowding the huge canvas that covered the east wall, Spencer's *The Resurrection of the Soldiers*. It always took me by surprise. I would spend an hour and a half or more in that small place, and I would have to return some six months later. Alas, I live much further away now. Another 'thin' place.

There are 'thin' moments, too, when time stands still, as we put it, and we hear the faint sound of the footsteps of God. I shall never forget a concert in Chester Town Hall, when the Lindsay String Quartet played one of Beethoven's late string quartets. When it came to the slow movement they played with their eyes closed. Something happened and we found ourselves on a different plane. The music was exquisite, the playing equally so, but they were not enough to explain it. It cannot be explained. It simply happened.

Nor shall I forget the afternoon some 25 years ago, when I stood on water meadows to the south of Salisbury and watched through my binoculars as a barn owl flew at eye height straight towards me. Binoculars focus the attention right down. The world becomes the small round space held by their lenses. There is nothing to distract. As the bird came closer, there was nothing I could see but the slow flap of its white wings, the disc of its face, and the large, round, black eyes looking into mine, until suddenly it registered I was there and swung away.

Much more remarkable still was the encounter between Bengt Berg, a Swedish bird photographer working in the early part of the twentieth century, and a bird called a dotterel. In his book *Min van fjallpiparen*, published in 1917, he describes how with utmost patience he managed to secure the bird's confidence. Dotterels are unusual as the males do the incubating of the eggs. They build a simple nest of grasses on the ground, and Berg had managed to find one. So trusting did the sitting bird become, that eventually it settled down on its eggs in the palm of Berg's hand. He had arranged some grass in his hand, and carefully arranged the eggs. The bird climbed on to his hand and then at once got off. There was something wrong. The eggs were not positioned quite right. So the bird rolled and turned them with his bill. Then he confidently climbed back on Berg's hand and settled down. He moved a few blades of grass with his bill, and then looked up into the man's face. 'Through the greenery in my hand,' Berg writes, 'I could feel his heart beating.' (The story is quoted by Staffan Söderblom in *Birds and Light: The Art of Lars Jonsson*, 2002, p. 22.)

And then there are 'thin' people, not thin in the usual sense, but people who remind us what it means to be human, and who take us beyond the human towards the divine. Just one example will do. When I was a curate I used to visit a Sarah Jones in the local psycho-geriatric hospital every fortnight and take her communion. When I first started going, I would find her in the day room, sitting next to her great friend, Mrs Wilshire. Then Sarah became too frail to be got out of bed. Often she would be in the ward by herself, or perhaps there would be an old man muttering to himself in a bed too far away for any conversation to be attempted. Sarah was a widow, but she had a son who lived not many miles from the town. I never heard of him coming to see her. She had a good deal of physical pain to put up with, also. Before we began the little service I would ask her what she wanted to pray for. Like a fool I thought each time she would say something about the pain in her back or her loneliness or her son. But she never asked me to pray for her. Always she would have something to tell me about one or more of the other patients and their particular needs. When finally I was about to leave the parish and came to see Sarah for the last time, I told her she had been an inspiration to me, and always would be. She looked at me with blank incomprehension. But I was right. Sarah Jones is still an inspiration to me. And of course, since then I have met other Sarahs, young and old, male as well as female, some whom I have met just the once, others I have been very close to for decades, who have reminded me of the intimacy of God, people who have been very good for me, who have opened my eyes to reality and its abiding mystery, who have shown me what matters and have helped me love a little more deeply. We all, please God, have our Sarah Joneses.

There is a verse in three of the Gospels that in the King James translation of Mark runs like this: 'And the veil of the temple was rent in twain from the top to the bottom' (Mark 15.38). Matthew's version in 27.51 is almost identical, Luke's a little simpler: 'and the veil of the temple was rent in the midst' (23.45b). In both Mark and Matthew the veil is torn as the crucified Jesus breathes his last and dies, in Luke immediately before that moment. This is figurative language. It is not to be taken literally. The high priest did not need to call in the needlewomen to make a quick repair. It means that with the death of Jesus God is out in the open. The veil, or the curtain in the sanctuary of the temple in Jerusalem, that hung across the Holy of Holies, is 'no longer there'. God is no longer locked away in a cupboard to which only the high priest has the key and which he will open but once a year. God has walked free, to roam the earth of his creating and call us all to join with him in the task of returning it to the state it was when he saw everything he had made and was able to declare without any hesitation or qualification that it was indeed 'very good' (Genesis 1.31).

And what a time to do it! What nonsense is this, that God comes out into the open at the very moment when the man who loves him so, who is so much of his mind and heart, who already has set so many free, who has made the last first, who has planted the Garden of Eden afresh in place after place, who has taken so many deep into God's territory, has sat them down in God's shade and washed their feet and fed them with God's food and drink, when *that* man *dies*? By itself it *is* a complete nonsense, and very nearly a blasphemy. But the story of Jesus' crucifixion does not stand alone. Jesus' story does not end with his death, it ends with his resurrection; or rather, with the resurrection it never ends and can never end. Without the resurrection, none of the Gospel writers would have spoken of the veil of the temple being torn down. As it is, that detail holds within its small compass a large part of the meaning and the truth not only of the crucifixion, but the resurrection, also.

With Jesus of Nazareth, and especially in his death, we find a human being and enter a place and a moment where talk of the veil between earth and heaven being thin is not enough. Instead we must speak of the veil being torn from top to bottom and left in a heap on the ground. The stories of Jesus' resurrection are, among other things, a way of putting that. They provide a commentary on that verse in Mark, Matthew and Luke. They take us inside a new Holy of Holies which has no walls or curtain round it; they make us linger in a strange moment of God's new making; they disclose to us the fullness of the truth of the human being, of the God who meets us there.

Thomas

I used to find the resurrection stories in the Gospels unsatisfactory. The crucifixion narratives were so superbly written, so sharp, yet so restrained. They took me to Golgotha, without overwhelming me with the horror of the place, and showed

me the God who hung there. Yet the resurrection stories somehow did not seem up to the job. I could not engage with them
in the same way, and Good Friday was often more moving for
me, a more profound occasion than Easter Sunday. Then one
particular story opened my eyes, and the rest fell obediently
into place. I knew where I was with them, and what I was
doing on Easter Sunday. They caught fire for me.

The story is in John's Gospel. I know full well the risks of in-
terpreting one Gospel, let alone three, in the light of another.
We have four Gospels in the New Testament, not one, and
each tells the story of Jesus of Nazareth in a distinct way. Each
has its own distinct tone and style; each has material not in
the other three. That is especially true of the beginnings and
ends of the Gospels. Matthew's narratives of the birth of Jesus
are different from Luke's, not just in detail, but in their mixture of light and shade. We may pretend in Christmas sermons or nativity plays that they tell one story, but they do
not. As for Mark, he has no stories of the birth of Jesus at all,
while John is content with his famous Prologue. At the other
end the resurrection stories also exhibit a large degree of diver-
sity. The story of the empty tomb is similar in Mark, Matthew
and Luke, and though John handles it in a quite distinctive
way, nevertheless it would seem he is relying on much the
same tradition. Beyond that, however, the Gospels largely go
their separate ways. In Mark's case, we are quite possibly deal-
ing with a truncated text, as we shall see, and his Gospel is
the only one not to include an encounter with the risen Jesus.
Matthew places his empty tomb story between two short
passages about the tomb being guarded by members of the
temple police. The stories of the walk to Emmaus and the
ascension of Christ are unique to Luke, while the much-loved
story of Mary of Magdala meeting the risen Christ in the
garden is only found in John, as are the story of Jesus' cook-
ing breakfast beside the Sea of Galilee, his dialogue with Peter,
and the story of Thomas.

And yet, at the risk of committing the sin of harmonizing
the Gospels, I would argue that we can find in John's dis-
tinctively Johannine story of Thomas a key to unlock all the

rest, not just the other resurrection stories in John, but those in Mark, Matthew and Luke as well.

We begin in the middle. The passage where Thomas meets the risen Christ is part of a larger unit that starts in John 20.19, straight after the story of Mary of Magdala. We will come to consider the rest of that unit in more detail in due course. Meanwhile a brief summary will suffice. The 'disciples' are gathered together in a house in Jerusalem, when Jesus suddenly appears in their midst. John tells us Jesus shows them his hands and his side, so grievously wounded by his crucifixion, speaks twice of peace, commissions them to continue with his work, and gives them the gift of the Spirit of God to enable them to carry it out. Who John has in mind when he talks of 'the disciples' here is not made entirely clear, though we can assume that Mary of Magdala was there. Thomas, however, is not among them.

> Now Thomas, one of the twelve, known as the Twin, was not with them when Jesus came. The other disciples kept saying to him, 'We have seen the Lord!' But he said to them, 'Unless I see the mark of the nails in his hands and put my finger in the mark of the nails and my hand in his side, I will not believe.'
>
> A week later his disciples were in the house once more, and this time Thomas was with them. Although the doors were locked, Jesus came and stood in the middle of them, and said, 'Peace be with you.' Then he said to Thomas, 'Put your finger here and see my hands; reach out your hand and put it in my side. Do not be unbelieving any more. Believe!' Thomas answered him and said, 'My Lord and my God!'
>
> Jesus said to him, 'Have you found belief because you have seen me? Blessed are those who have not seen but yet believe.' (John 20.24–29)

This is the climax to his Gospel, and indeed John brings the whole work to a conclusion in the next two verses: 'Now of course Jesus performed many other signs in the presence of his disciples, which are not written in this book. But these are written that you might believe that Jesus is the Messiah, the Son of God, and that through believing you may have life in his name' (20.30–31). (In the Gospel as we have it, this turns out not to be the end. There is another chapter to come, probably written by the same author as an afterthought, possibly by a second person whose thought and style were very similar.) Yet despite the fact that Thomas' story occupies such a place in the Gospel, John nearly ruins it. When I taught at Salisbury and Wells Theological College, I ran a short course encouraging students to have a go at writing a sermon in the form of a story. 'When you get to the end of the story,' I said to them, 'stop and say no more. Resist the temptation, if it comes, to explain or sum up, or "give the message". After all, stories cannot be reduced to messages.' The students often produced remarkable work, and the vast majority heeded my advice. Just occasionally, however, someone would feel compelled to draw 'the moral' of the story at the end. Invariably, when we came to them reading their pieces to one another, that person would not need to be told they had spoiled the effect. It was obvious in everyone's reactions; they knew it for themselves.

Now the best of the Bible's storytelling refuses to explain itself or make comment. We are given the story and that is that. Just think, for example, of the Garden of Eden story in Genesis 2—3, or Jesus' Parable of the Father and the Two Lost Sons (usually, but misleadingly, called the Parable of the Prodigal Son) in Luke 15.11–32. These are highly sophisticated tales, many-layered and of extraordinary profundity. Yet we are not invited by the author of Genesis or by Luke or Jesus to *understand* them, so much as enter upon their strange and wonderful territories and be changed by them. Each is like a walled garden that we must walk into and wander about in and sit down and close our eyes and listen and smell, then open our eyes again and see and notice and feel and touch, and emerge once more into the world outside different from when we went in.

John is a superb storyteller, but I cannot help thinking I would have had much to say to him if he had been in my class at Salisbury and Wells! And of his Thomas story I would have said, 'Oh no, John, don't spoil it! Add verses 30 and 31, of course, to bring your whole great work to an end, but leave Thomas' cry "My Lord and my God" hanging in the air. You can't follow that! Don't crowd out its echo by some remark about seeing and believing! Oh, I can see what you are trying to do. You are having Jesus address the people of your own day, those who belong to the generation after those who knew him in the flesh and went round with him in Jerusalem and Galilee. You are using him to tell them their belief is of no less worth, just because they were not there themselves; indeed, perhaps it is more to be commended because they have not had the advantage the first disciples had. Oh, I understand that, I agree with it, but don't you see what you've done? You've ended your extraordinary story by preaching at us. You keep doing this, John, all the way through your Gospel. You keep popping up and telling us what to think. Let us think and feel for ourselves! The trouble is, John, that when people hear your story of Thomas, they won't remember his extraordinary declaration. All they'll think of is Jesus' telling him off. No doubt, he'll be "doubting Thomas" for the rest of his days!'

But plenty of people *have* noticed Thomas' declaration, of course, even though they may not have been nearly as hard on John as I have just been. His 'My Lord and my God!' looks back to the very beginning of the Gospel, whose Prologue contains these words:

In the beginning was the Word, and the Word was with God, and the Word was God . . . He was in the world, and the world came into being through him; yet the world did not know him . . . And the Word became flesh and pitched his tent among us, and we have seen his glory, the glory as of the Father's only son, full of grace and truth . . . No one has ever seen God. It is God the only Son, the one so close to the Father's heart, who has made him known. (1.1, 10, 14, 18)

Though first John the Baptist (1.34), then Nathanael (1.49) and later Martha (11.27) declare that Jesus is 'the Son of God', and though Peter, speaking for the Twelve, says to him, 'We have come to believe and know that you are the Holy One of God,' (6.69), yet N. T. Wright is correct when looking back to 1.18 in particular he writes,

> We watch in vain, throughout the rest of the gospel, for characters in the story to wake up to what is going on. Jesus 'reveals his glory' to the disciples in various ways, but nobody responds with anything that matches what is said in 1.18. Until Easter . . . The so-called 'Doubting Thomas' takes one small verbal step and a giant leap of faith and theology: 'My lord and my god.' This at last is faith indeed.
>
> (*The Resurrection of the Son of God*, 2003, p. 668)

But see who it is who Thomas calls 'My Lord and my God'! A figure bearing the marks of crucifixion. We have a wounded God here, a God who bears the marks not just of human rejection, but of careful, deliberate humiliation and terrible brutality. It is utterly astonishing. Never in the history of religions has such a claim been made, or such a vision been had. No wonder we find these resurrection stories hard to come to terms with.

John may well have been writing his Gospel during the reign of the Roman Emperor Domitian (81–96). Domitian was called 'Our Lord and God', and no doubt was delighted with the titles. To proclaim Jesus 'Lord and God' was to challenge Domitian. As John Dominic Crossan has put it: 'The first-century question is not "Do you think Jesus is Lord?" It is "Do you think Caesar or Jesus is Lord?" and when you say, "Jesus is Lord," you have just committed high treason' (*The Resurrection of Jesus: The Crossan–Wright Dialogue*, ed. Robert B. Stewart, 2006, p. 28).

So Thomas in John's story commits high treason, and with the most astonishing bravado, too. It is as if he comes into Domitian's throne room without knocking, without bowing or waiting for an invitation to speak, and says, 'Mr Ex-emperor, may I present the new emperor to you. He doesn't have your fine trappings of power, I'm afraid. In fact, when you look at him, you'll see he's just been crucified as a criminal. He's what you would call the scum of the earth. Well, Mr Ex-emperor, he's actually "your Lord and your God", and ours too, of course – of the whole world, naturally. I'm sorry he's not a more presentable God, but that's not exactly his fault.'

But the Hebrew background to Thomas' words is more remarkable still. It is that that makes them the climax to the whole of John's great work, and the key to the rest of the resurrection stories. For 'Lord and God' brings together the two most commonly used titles for God of the Hebrew Scriptures, where behind the term 'Lord' stands the mysterious, unpronounceable divine name YHWH. The first time the Bible combines them both is in the Garden of Eden story in Genesis 2—3. Thomas, or John if you prefer, takes us back to Eden, to the place where we human beings grew up too fast (so that story goes), and where, suddenly knowing far too much, we became afraid and hid ourselves from the God who made us:

> And they heard the sound of the Lord God walking about in the garden in the evening breeze, and the human and his woman hid from the Lord God in the midst of the trees of the garden. And the Lord God called to the human and said to him, 'Where are you?' And he said, 'I heard your sound in the garden and I was afraid, for I was naked, and I hid.'
>
> (Genesis 3.8–10, Robert Alter's translation)

That dialogue is one of the most tragic in the whole Bible, for it marks not just a loss of innocence, but a loss of intimacy, of that easy, natural, fear-less relationship with a God who walks in his garden in the evening breeze, and whose sound is mysteriously audible to human ears.

Thomas' cry 'My Lord and my God!' return us to Eden and to that ancient intimacy with God we thought we had lost forever. And that helps to explain why the God who meets him is described in such physical terms. We need them, of course, to convey the vision of a wounded God, scarred with the nails and spear of crucifixion. But such physical language applied to God is also the language of intimacy, language that both describes it and creates it. In Eden, God shapes a human being from the dust, puffs the life into the creature's nostrils, plants a garden, speaks without any prior formality, allows us to hear what is going through his mind, acts as surgeon and healer, walks to and fro so that the humans, now a couple, can hear him coming, engages them in dialogue, and even becomes tailor and makes them clothes. Such language used to be thought naïve, and sometimes it still is. But the Eden story is one of the most sophisticated and complex in the entire Bible. The storyteller knew well what he was doing. Of course he did not mean his language to be taken literally. There is, after all, nothing we can say of God that can be taken literally. The author of Genesis was using language drawn unashamedly from the human sphere in order to create an impression of familiarity. It is as if he is saying, 'Once upon a time there was no distance between us human beings and God. We lived in his garden and met him there every day. We could talk with him as we talk to our neighbour, for he *was* our neighbour, and we were his. This is the intimacy with which we were made. This is the intimacy for which we were made.'

There is, of course, an unbearable pathos about the Eden story, because it ends with the human couple being expelled from the garden and driven into a world where meeting God will be more problematic. It is no accident that the language of Eden hardly ever reappears. But on occasion it does, later in Genesis and in the Moses stories in Exodus. Of all the stories of encounter with God in the Hebrew Scriptures the most mysterious is the one about Jacob wrestling with him through the dark hours of the night at the wadi Jabbok (Genesis 32.22–32). The storyteller's daring is without parallel here, for early in the passage he tells of Jacob being a match for God and of God begging him to let him go. True, we do not have a wounded God at the Jabbok. It is Jacob, not God, who leaves the scene with a limp. Yet never again do the Hebrew Scriptures speak so boldly, so profoundly of God's vulnerability.

There are hints of it elsewhere, however, in the Moses stories among other places. In Exodus there are two extraordinary statements exactly one chapter apart. In Exodus 33.11, we find this: 'And the Lord would speak to Moses face to face, as one speaks to a friend', and in Exodus 32.11 (if we translate the Hebrew literally) this: 'And Moses soothed the face of the Lord his God.' I know of only one translator of Exodus 32.11 who dares to reproduce the Hebrew, and he is Everett Fox in his *The Five Books of Moses*. Even Robert Alter, who usually has such a feel for the language and such a mastery of it, has, 'And Moses implored the presence of the Lord his God', and such a translation is far more typical. Alas, it drains the Hebrew of its beauty, its poetry and its power, and makes it into something humdrum and dull. It does not matter that the phrase to 'soothe someone's face' is a fairly stock one. Common or not, it gains in such a context extraordinary potency, and in its very few words sums up all that the relationship between Moses and God means. We do not come across such intimacy, such familiarity with God again, not until we reach the Gospels.

Yet we need to say more about John's way of talking in the Thomas story. He is trying to convey the great truth that, in the risen Christ, God is very close and once more familiar. And he wishes to present us with the image of a wounded God. But does he really need to speak of Jesus inviting Thomas to touch him, to reach out and put his finger on the marks of the nails and on the spear's wound? Surely that is going too far. We will more easily feel the shock of it, perhaps, if we transfer this Jesus from the Roman Empire of the first century to Hitler's Reich of the twentieth. We then have to imagine Jesus pointing to the number indelibly imprinted on his arm, the number he was given in the concentration camp before he was led to the gas chamber. What could such language possibly mean, the invitation to touch and feel? Is Jesus speaking ironically, as Robert Morgan suggests (*Resurrection: Essays in Honour of Leslie Houlden*, eds Stephen Barton and Graham Stanton, 1994, p. 10), or even sarcastically, as Raymond Brown has it in the second volume of his Anchor Bible Commentary on John, *The Gospel According to John* (XIII–XXI) (1970, p. 1046)? There is irony there, surely, because no one can touch God. But no one can see God or hear God, either, though such language, so familiar to us, does not unnerve us so much, because it keeps God still at a certain distance. To 'touch' God is to do away with the distance altogether, and that might seem to mean to do away with the otherness of God, the sheer Godness of God, and reduce him to our level.

Some second-century commentators on John's story did go too far. Ignatius tells us the disciples, 'touched him and believed'; the *Epistula Apostolorum* says Peter touched the marks of the nails and Thomas touched the wound left by the spear, while Andrew saw the footprints that Jesus left behind him (see Brown's commentary, vol. 2, p. 1046). These writers are trying their best to demonstrate that the risen Christ was 'real', but in fact they turn John's story into bathos, and empty his risen Christ of meaning. They try too hard and spoil everything. If you are going to use human language of God, you must do so with great skill. The writers of Genesis and Exodus knew exactly how to do it, how to bring God close and make him familiar, while still preserving a sense of mystery. It can be a matter of simply a phrase, a few words that separate the sublime from the ridiculous.

In John's story, Thomas does *not* touch Jesus, nor does John make clear whether he could if he tried – hence Morgan's talk of 'irony' and Brown's of 'sarcasm'. And yet the question remains: does John go too far in telling of the invitation to touch?

Dale Allison's *Resurrecting Jesus* (2005, pp. 269–99) contains a fascinating discussion of apparitions of the dead. He speaks of the moving experiences he himself and members of his family have had (see pp. 275–7), and among the myriad of other cases he reports is this testimony of a woman who believed she encountered her dead husband, and on two occasions:

> He looked and felt just like when he was living. He didn't look like something you could see through, neither time. He just looked real, alive, real. I put my arms around him, it felt just like you or I, just real. You know like, the Lord reappeared, you know when he died, and he was alive and he asked the man to feel the nail hole in his side. My husband was just as real as if he was there with me now. (*Resurrecting Jesus*, p. 291)

Allison refers to well-researched reports of apparitions of the same person appearing to several people at once or at different times, or where the apparition has spoken and conveyed information not otherwise available, or where people have seen an apparition of someone they did not know had died (see pp. 294–5). He lists testimonies of those, like the woman who had lost her husband, for whom the apparition seemed 'solid and firm', 'warm and full of life', able to embrace and kiss, or to be touched (p. 281, n. 327). He is careful not to claim too much, and certainly he does not suggest that such experiences prove the truth of the resurrection of Jesus, or its character. Nevertheless, he may be right that the *language* of the resurrection stories owes something to the human experience of apparitions of the dead. For the Thomas story in John is not the only one where the risen Christ is spoken of in physical terms. Like an apparition of the dead he can pass through locked doors, or appear and disappear. He can also walk and talk, break bread, cook breakfast and eat; he can have his feet grasped and be mistaken for a gardener.

Yet, as Wright has emphasized, such apparitions are apparitions of the *dead*, reminders to those who receive them that the people they encounter really are dead (*The Resurrection of Jesus: John Dominic Crossan and NT Wright in Dialogue*, p. 35). The resurrection stories in the Gospels are not accounts of his friends' experiences of Jesus as an apparition. If that were the case, then he would simply have joined the great multitude of those who have appeared to others after their deaths. His appearances would no doubt have meant a great deal to those who received them, and they would have remembered them for the rest of their lives. But once they themselves had died, Jesus and his memory would have died with them, and no Christian communities would have sprung up in the meantime.

John's story of Thomas reminds us that the encounters with the risen Jesus, received by a number of people (some of whose names we know) at particular times and in particular places, made and still make such an impact, because they were and are encounters with God. With the risen Jesus, his friends found themselves in the presence of God. It was as simple, as profound, as shattering and as life-changing as that.

This God was both familiar and a stranger. It is no accident that some of the stories speak of the friends not immediately recognizing him. He was familiar, because he was somehow the same as the man from Nazareth they knew and loved so well. He was a stranger, because he was God, because he was the Beyond, the Other, the Mystery whose face is veiled . . . or has been hitherto.

That explains why the resurrection stories do not conform to the expectations that people then held of life after death. Wright goes to great lengths to establish this point (see the first part of his *The Resurrection of the Son of God*, pp. 3–206). Apparitions of the dead may very well convince people at the profoundest possible level that the ones they loved and still love have some kind of life after death, and much more than the shadowy existence of a ghost (as Allison points out, experiences of apparitions are not the same as encounters with ghosts – *Resurrecting Jesus*, p. 290). Yet, when the disciples met the risen Jesus, they were not merely reassured that he was enjoying a life after death.

Nor did they believe that he had simply come back to life. The stories the Gospel writers tell of the resurrection are not like those of Jesus raising people from the dead: Jairus' daughter (Mark 5.21–43 and parallels), or the son of an unnamed widow of Nain (Luke 7.11–17), or his friend Lazarus (John 11.1–44). Whether or not we believe Jesus really did bring those people back from the dead, their stories describe him bringing them back to this life where, we would hope, Jairus' daughter will marry and have children (that, at least, is what her family will want for her), the young man in Nain will look after his mother (as she and the people of Nain will expect), and Lazarus will resume his place in the family. Jairus' daughter and the son of the widow of Nain are both one-scene characters and we do not hear of either of them again. However, John does take Lazarus' story a step further, and tells us of a meal Jesus has with the family when Lazarus is present (12.1–2), and then of a plot of the chief priests to kill Lazarus, since he is provoking such an interest in the man who brought him back to life (12.9–11). This last detail is illuminating. One day, please God not through any violence (tantalizingly, John

does not mention Lazarus again, though some scholars identify him with the beloved disciple), Lazarus will die once more.
Jesus has shown he is the master of death (all three stories
about him raising someone from the dead are making that
claim), but one day Lazarus, like Jairus' daughter and the
widow's son, will die as we all do.

The stories of the resurrection of Jesus are not about a man
brought back to life, who can and will die again. They are
about a man who has burst out of death into the very life of
God, who through the very nature of his death – think of the
marks of nail and spear – shows us God. They are about a
man of whom we say, when we look him in the face, 'My Lord
and my God!' – and our view of him, and our view of God
is then never the same again.

The curtain is drawn aside

There are other stories in the Gospels that prepare the way
for the resurrection stories and for Thomas and his great declaration. They are not themselves resurrection stories. You
cannot have a resurrection story without a death preceding
it. Yet some of their details will reappear in the resurrection
stories, sufficient to invite us to make a link between them.
And when we reach the resurrection stories we can more
easily hear what is being said, if we look back to these earlier
episodes. They are not stories where the veil is torn in two
from top to bottom, but rather ones where the curtain is
drawn aside for a moment, and we look into the Holy of
Holies and gain a glimpse of God.

We will consider briefly just four of them: the story of the
transfiguration, the stories of the calming of the storm and
the walking on the sea, and the feeding of the five thousand.

The transfiguration story occurs in Matthew, Mark and
Luke. This is Matthew's version of it:

Six days later, Jesus took Peter and James and his brother
John and led them up a high mountain by themselves.
And he was transfigured before them, and his face shone
like the sun, and his clothes became white as the light.

19

And behold Moses and Elijah appeared to them, talking with him. Peter answered and said to Jesus, 'Lord, it is good for us to be here. If you wish I will make three tents, one for you, one for Moses, and one for Elijah.' While he was speaking a cloud full of light overshadowed them, and behold a voice came from the cloud saying, 'This is my Son, the Beloved; with him I am well pleased. Listen to him!' When the disciples heard that, they prostrated themselves and were overcome with fear. But Jesus came, touched them and said, 'Arise, do not be afraid.' When they looked up, they saw no one, except Jesus all on his own.   (Matthew 17.1–8)

Many Christian pilgrims to the Holy Land are taken to Mount Tabor and are told it was the site of the transfiguration. Impressive though Tabor is, it is not a high mountain, nor even a low one. It is but a hill rising out of the plain of Jezreel. You might think they would do better looking to the north, to Mount Hermon, which reaches to 9,232 feet and is often covered in snow. But they would still be looking to the wrong place. For neither Matthew nor Mark nor Luke gives the mountain a name. They refuse to try to pin it down, for they know that is impossible. What I said of the site of the burning bush in *Face to Face with God* applies here also: 'We are in mysterious country, beyond the edges of maps, beyond human knowledge, nearly beyond human imagining. We have entered upon the very mystery of God.'

Yet all three Gospel writers do have the rich memories of a particular mountain in mind, Mount Sinai, the place where Moses 'soothed the face of the Lord his God', where the Lord would speak to him 'face to face', and where, so Exodus 24.9–11 tells us: 'Moses went up, and with him Aaron, Nadab, and Abihu and seventy of the elders of Israel. And they saw the God of Israel, and beneath his feet was like a fashioning of sapphire pavement and like the very heavens for pureness... and they beheld God and ate and drank' (Robert Alter's translation, from *The Five Books of Moses*, pp. 457–8). Later in that same passage Moses goes up to the summit of the mountain to receive God's teaching, and we read,

Moses went up, and the cloud covered the mountain. And the Lord's glory settled on Mount Sinai, and the cloud covered it for six days; on the seventh day he called out to Moses from the midst of the cloud. And the appearance of the Lord's glory was like consuming fire on the top of the mountain before the eyes of the Israelites. And Moses entered within the cloud. (24.15–18a)

Ten chapters later Moses comes down the mountain and we hear that, 'the skin of his face shone because he had been talking with God. When Aaron and all the Israelites saw Moses, behold the skin of his face was shining, and they were afraid to come near him. But Moses called to them' (34.29b–31a).

These short quotations are enough to tell us how to approach the story of Jesus' transfiguration, though there is one more we should give, the opening words of a vision of God from the book of Daniel:

As I watched,
thrones were set in place,
and an Ancient One took his throne;
his clothing was as white as snow,
and the hair of his head like pure wool.
(Daniel 7.9)

In the transfiguration story we step into the circle of the divine. It is not just Peter, James and John who are there. The Gospel writers take us with them, and the scales fall from our eyes also. We do not have to wait till we hear God speak. Every detail, the mountain, the select little band climbing to its summit, Jesus' face and clothes blazing with light, the mysterious cloud with its shadow wondrously full of light, even the six days at the start that might seem at first to add nothing to the sense, these all remind us that we are deep in the presence of God. Here we see behind the scenes. Here we grasp the truth of what is going on, what this Jesus from Nazareth means and who he is.

We find a Jesus who is a new Moses, yes, but who is much more than that. Moses' face in Exodus 34 reflects the glory of God as a mirror catching the blinding sun. On the mount of

21

the transfiguration Jesus *is* the glory of God. The light shines
not off him, but from him, and is the same as the light that
fills the cloud. In Mark's version of the story the three disciples are overcome with awe and fear before the cloud
overshadows them and they hear God speaking; for them the
vision of the transfigured Jesus is enough by itself (see Mark
9.6).

When we reach the resurrection stories, we do not find a
risen Jesus blazing with light, outshining the sun, though some
like the great Rembrandt have so depicted him. Those stories
take us even deeper into the heart of God, where no language
will do. None of the four Gospel writers attempts to describe
the overwhelming moment of Jesus' resurrection. His friends
meet him after the event. But the women at Jesus' tomb in
Matthew 28.3 do encounter an angel whose appearance is 'like
lightning' and whose clothing is as 'white as snow'; in Mark
16.5 they find an angel 'dressed in a white robe'; in Luke 24.4
two angels in 'dazzling clothes'; in John 20.12 'two angels in
white'. We are in the same territory as before.

In Matthew the women experience a similar mixture of
emotions as the three other disciples at the transfiguration.
On the unnamed, nameless mountain of the transfiguration,
Peter and his friends are overcome with fear, and yet Peter
cries, 'It is good to be here!' and tries to capture and hold on
to the vision by building not one tent of meeting, as Exodus
33.7 calls it, but three. So the women at the tomb are overcome with both fear and joy (Matthew 28.8), while in John's
story of Mary of Magdala meeting with the risen Jesus she
will try to hold on to him.

At the very end of Matthew's story, when the risen Jesus
gives his disciples their final commission to carry on and
extend his work, he does so on a mountain (28.16).

Luke concludes his transfiguration story with the words,
'And they kept silent and in those days told no one anything
of what they had seen' (Luke 9.36b). 'Those days' means the
period before the resurrection and their encounter with the
risen Jesus. Both Matthew and Mark, as they reach the end of
their versions of the story, make the reference to the resurrection explicit: 'As they were coming down the mountain,

Jesus ordered them, "Tell no one of the vision until after the Son of Man has been raised from the dead" ' (Matthew 17.1–9; Mark 9.9 is very similar). To encounter the risen Christ is to penetrate the mystery of the transfiguration; to stand there with Peter, James and John on the mountain of the transfiguration means we more easily recognize where we are when we meet the risen Christ. We are in the presence of God.

And so we are when a storm is suddenly calmed, or when Jesus comes walking over the surface of the sea, or when a huge crowd of people with nothing to eat are given so much food they cannot finish it all and for a short time the disciples are left with a litter problem.

The story of Jesus calming a storm on the Sea of Galilee occurs in Matthew, Mark and Luke, the companion story of his walking on the sea in Matthew, Mark and John. Mark's version of the calming of the storm goes like this: Jesus has been teaching a crowd of people beside the Sea of Galilee, and the day is coming to an end. He says to his closest disciples, 'Let us go across to the other side' (Mark 4.35). More literally, and perhaps more powerfully, we could translate, 'Let us go into the beyond.' They get on board a boat, and set out for the far shore, leaving the crowd behind.

> And a furious storm arose and the waves rushed into the boat, so that the boat was already being swamped. But he was in the stern, asleep on the cushion. And they roused him and said to him, 'Teacher, is it nothing to you that we are perishing?' Waking up he rebuked the wind and said to the sea, 'Be quiet! Let your jaws be muzzled!' And the wind grew weary and there was a great calm.
>
> (Mark 4.37–9; compare Matthew 8.24–6; Luke 8.23–4)

Two chapters later we reach the story of the walking on the water. This time Jesus has been feeding a huge crowd beside the sea, and again he tells his disciples to get into a boat and set sail for the far shore (the same phrase 'into the beyond' is used, but now its meaning is mundane, for Mark adds 'to Bethsaida'). This time, however, Jesus does not get into the

23

boat with them, but stays behind to dismiss the crowd, and then climbs a mountain to pray.

> Evening came and the boat was in the middle of the sea, while he was alone on the land. He saw them straining at the oars against an adverse wind, and about the fourth watch of the night he came towards them walking on the sea. He intended to pass them by. But when they saw him walking on the sea, they thought it was a ghost, and they cried out; for they all saw him and were terrified. But immediately he spoke to them and said, 'Take heart! I am! Do not be afraid!' Then he got into the boat with them, and the wind grew weary.
>
> (Mark 6.47–51a; compare Matthew 14.23b–32;
> John 6.17b–21)

Both these stories are packed full of references to the Hebrew Scriptures and cannot be properly understood without them. These are not 'impossible' events to encourage the sceptical to dismiss the Bible as fanciful and childish. Nor do they 'prove' that Jesus must have been divine, because he performed such feats before breakfast. Those who take either of those positions miss the symbolism of the stories, and look only at their surface.

They are not stories for children, not young children at least. They both happen in the dark, and concern a terrifying contest with the forces of evil and chaos. The violent storm in the first one is no ordinary one, but has a demonic presence. It is like a great monster threatening to devour the boat and all those within it in its jaws. That is why I have translated the Greek of Mark 4.39 so literally: Jesus 'rebukes' the wind, tells the sea to 'be quiet', ordering it to 'be muzzled', and finally the wind 'grows weary'. The myth of the struggle of the creator gods with a great sea monster was widespread in the ancient Near East, and predated the formation of Israelite theology. Occasionally that myth breaks the surface of the text of the Hebrew Bible:

> Awake, awake, put on strength,
> O arm of the LORD!

Awake, as in days of old,
the generations of long ago!
Was it not you who cut Rahab in pieces,
who pierced the dragon?
Was it not you who dried up the sea,
the waters of the great deep;
who made the depths of the sea a way
for the redeemed to cross over?

(Isaiah 51.9–10)

The dragon is called Rahab here, and the poet uses ancient creation language to describe what was in his tradition God's supreme act of salvation, his bringing his people safely across the Red Sea and defeating the Egyptian forces that threatened to destroy them. In Exodus 14, where the story of that crossing is told, the account is demythologized. When the Red Sea is cut in two, the writer does not talk about the sea monster being sliced in half, let alone 'cut in pieces', but God's power to control the sea and the wind is still clearly asserted. The poets of the psalms, like the writer of Isaiah 51, are less cautious:

You rule the raging of the sea;
when its waves rise, you still them.
You crushed Rahab like a carcass;
you scattered your enemies with your mighty arm.

(Psalm 89.9–10)

Here Rahab refers again both to the sea monster of ancient myth and to the Egyptian forces of the pharaoh of the oppression, and the writer of Psalm 106.9 also has them in mind when he says of God: 'He rebuked the Red Sea, and it became dry.'

Psalm 104.5–7a has the creation itself in view:

You set the earth on its foundations,
so that it shall never be shaken.
You cover it with the deep as with a garment;
the waters stood above the mountains.
At your rebuke they flee.

25

In the Greek Septuagint translation of both of those last passages, the word used for 'rebuke' is the same, or from the same root, as the one Mark (followed by Matthew and Luke) has in his story of the calming of the storm.

Verses from Psalm 77 remind us of both the calming of the storm and the walking on the water, while a further verse describing God from the book of Job brings out the mythological background to the second:

> When the waters saw you, O God,
> when the waters saw you and were convulsed;
> the very deep trembled . . .
> Your way was through the sea,
> your path through the mighty waters
> yet your footprints could not be seen.
>   (Psalm 77.16, 19, my translation)

> He alone stretches out the heavens,
> and tramples upon the sea monster's back.
>   (Job 9.8, David Cline's translation,
>   *Job 1—20*, 1989)

In other places where the sea is drained of mythology, but still highly dangerous, God is celebrated as the one who can control it. The description of the sea in Psalm 107 is justly famous and includes the verses:

> Then they cried to the LORD in their trouble,
> and he brought them out of their distress;
> he made the storm be still,
> and the waves of the sea were hushed.
>   (vv. 28–9)

Then there is the playful passage near the beginning of the story of Jonah, where God is able to do whatever he likes with sea and storm.

So the stories in the Gospels of Jesus calming the storm or walking on the sea present him as the Master of the forces of chaos and evil. They present him quite simply as God. As we have seen, some of the poets in the Hebrew Bible apply the language of the myth of the divine struggle with the sea to the Israelites' crossing of the Red Sea. It is interesting to compare the Moses of Exodus 14 with the Jesus of the Gospel stories. Moses also tells the terrified Israelites to 'take heart' (Exodus 14.13; the Septuagint has exactly the same Greek word as Mark in 6.50, or Matthew in 14.27). But Moses acts on a command from God and under his precise instructions. To control the sea, he uses a staff that is charged with the authority and power of God. The splitting of the sea, or its being driven back by a fierce wind, is God's doing, not his. He is simply God's servant, obeying his orders. Jesus on the Sea of Galilee needs no command from God, no instructions, no staff. He himself rebukes and muzzles the forces of evil, or strides through the dark across the back of the sea, as only God can. In Matthew's version of the walking on the water, Peter calls out to Jesus as he approaches the boat and begins to walk towards him on the surface of the waves. But then as he starts to sink, he cries out to Jesus to save him. 'Immediately,' Matthew says, 'Jesus reached out his hand and caught him' (14.31). When we hear the poet of Psalm 144.7 address God with the words,

> Stretch out your hand from on high;
> set me free and rescue me from the mighty waters,

then we realize that, even in the seemingly simple action of reaching out his hand to Peter, Jesus is doing what God does. No wonder then that in all three versions of the walking on the water Jesus greets his friends with the words, 'I am' (Mark 6.50; Matthew 14.27; John 6.20), words that find their roots in the story of the burning bush. There Moses asks God to reveal his name. The Hebrew of God's reply in Exodus 3.14 is ambiguous and in fact amounts to a playful refusal to give him what he asks. Nevertheless, it is often translated 'I am who I am', and in the Septuagint is rendered, 'I am the One who is.' For Jesus to say 'I am' is not simply to say 'Don't worry, it's me.' It is to use the language of divinity, to reassure his friends that they are in the presence of God himself, and that is why they have nothing to fear.

These stories anticipate the stories of the resurrection in that they too draw the curtain to one side and let us see what is really going on. Everything in the Gospels is meant to show us God, and show us God in the person of Jesus of Nazareth. The transfiguration, the calming of the storm, the walking on the water and the resurrection are all key moments when that is made plain, and the stories of the resurrection hold the key to the rest: without the resurrection, without the disciples' experience of meeting Jesus the other side of his death and encountering him as God, those earlier stories would never have been written. Much of Jesus' teaching might have been preserved, many of his healings remembered, the ways in which he turned so many things upside down – and I do not mean just the tables of the money changers in the temple – might have continued for a time to have an impact on his friends, but that would have been all. There would have been no Gospels, no gospel.

The calming of the storm and the walking on the water also anticipate the ultimate triumph of God over the forces of evil and destruction that the resurrection of Jesus represents. Yet that is precisely why their victory can seem too straight-forward, too easy. In God's second great speech in Job 40.6—41.34 he tells Job of his ongoing struggle with the monsters Behemoth and Leviathan. They, like Rahab in Isaiah 51 or Psalm 89, are drawn from the world of dark mythology, and are the cause of terror and suffering on the earth, such as Job himself has been enduring for so long. Yet neither of them in Job 40—41 is cut in pieces or crushed like a carcass. They are not invincible, but they are so terrifying that God himself must draw his sword before he approaches them (Job 40.19). One might say the vision of that poem is more realistic, more redolent of the world in which we live and of the one with which God has to deal. Yet, of course, the Gospels do not come to the stories of the resurrection until they have spoken of Jesus' arrest, of his trials, of his being mocked and flogged, of his stumbling through the streets of Jerusalem bearing his own cross, of nails and spear, of strange, cloying darkness, and of death. In the end, the end of each of the Gospels, the triumph of God comes at enormous cost, as Thomas can see from the wounds still showing on Jesus' risen body.

Before we return to those resurrection stories, we must visit briefly the story of the feeding of the five thousand. The resurrection is not just about God's triumph over evil and death. As we have seen, it is also about the recovery of that ancient intimacy with God, the easy familiarity all too briefly enjoyed in the Garden of Eden. Some of the most profound stories or poems reflecting on encounter with God in the Hebrew Bible concern hospitality and the sharing of a meal. We have already quoted one of them, the scene in Exodus 24, when Moses and others feast with God on the summit of Mount Sinai. Two of the resurrection stories will speak of meals with the risen Jesus. The feeding of the five thousand (together with the additional stories of the feeding of the four thousand in Mark and Matthew) is yet another story of encounter with God that anticipates the climax of the resurrection.

It is the only one of Jesus' miracles to be found in all four Gospels, and in Matthew and Mark comes immediately before the walking on the water (Matthew 14.13–21; Mark 6.30–44; Luke 9.10–17; John 6.1–15). In Matthew's case it would be better named the feeding of the (perhaps) twenty thousand (and possibly many more), because he talks of a crowd of 'about five thousand men, besides women and children' (14.21). Matthew and Mark speak of it happening in 'a deserted place' (Matthew 14.13; Mark 6.32); John locates it on an unnamed mountain (6.3).

Why is the crowd there? On that all four Gospels agree: they have followed Jesus because of their great need. They have seen what Jesus has been doing, and they need him. Matthew, Luke and John make particular mention of their having seen him healing the sick. The term Matthew uses for 'sick' in 14.14 means 'powerless', and the different word describing them in John 6.2 means 'weak'. Mark and Matthew say that Jesus was filled with compassion as soon as he saw them, and Mark adds, 'because they were like sheep without a shepherd' (6.34). That phrase makes us even more keenly aware of their vulnerability. In Palestine, then as now, sheep could not be left in the fields with occasional visits from the shepherd. They had to be continuously supervised, led to the best grazing and to where water could be found. There were wolves, lions and bears to contend with. John's Jesus, in his picture of 'the good shepherd', talks of the risk that a shepherd runs of losing his life in protecting his sheep (10.11). Sheep without a shepherd would themselves not survive.

In a passage of great power the prophet Ezekiel denounces the kings of Israel for serving their own interests at the expense of the people. In accordance with ancient custom, common throughout the ancient Near East, he calls these kings 'shepherds'.

> Ah, you shepherds of Israel who have been feeding your-selves! Should not shepherds feed the sheep? You eat the fat, you clothe yourselves with the wool, you slaughter the fatlings; but you do not feed the sheep. You have not strengthened the weak, you have not healed the sick, you have not bound up the injured, you have not brought back the strayed, you have not sought the lost, but with force and harshness you have ruled them. So they were scattered, because there was no shepherd; and scattered, they became food for all the wild animals . . . Thus says the LORD God: I myself will search for my sheep, and will seek them out . . . I will feed them with good pas-ture . . . I will seek the lost, and I will bring back the strayed, and I will bind up the injured, and I will strengthen the weak . . . I will feed them with justice.
>
> (Ezekiel 34.2b–5, 11, 14, 16)

The feeding of the five thousand sums up the meaning of all that Jesus does. In him we see God at work, we see God taking over from the rulers and the landowners who keep the peasants in poverty and tax some of them into slavery, and who ensure they have no power to change things. We see God establish his own kingdom, his own empire. In Isaiah we have a vision of that kingdom:

> On this mountain the LORD of hosts will make for all
>   peoples
> a feast of rich food, a feast of well-matured wines,
> of rich food filled with marrow,

of well-matured wines strained clear . . .
he will swallow up death for ever.
Then the LORD God will wipe away the tears from all
    faces.

(25.6, 8a)

In the Gospels there are several sayings and parables that speak
of the nature of God's reign or its final establishment in similar terms. Think of the feast in the Parable of the Father and
the Two Lost Sons in Luke 15.11–32, or of the Parable of the
Great Dinner in Luke 14.15–23, with its parallel in Matthew
22.1–14, where the meal becomes a wedding banquet. Think
of the astonishing passage in Luke 12.35–37, where Jesus says,

> Keep your aprons on and your lamps burning! Be like
> those who await their master at whatever hour he returns
> from the wedding party, prepared to open for him as
> soon as he arrives and knocks. Blessed are those servants
> whom the master finds on the alert when he arrives!
> Believe me, he will put on an apron, make them recline
> at table, and will come and serve them.

(Joseph Fitzmyer's translation,
The Gospel According to Luke X–XXIV, 1983)

With the feeding of the five thousand the curtain is drawn
aside, and we look into heaven. True, there is no feast of rich
food and well-aged wines. Bread and fish are the staple food
of the fishermen and peasant families who live round the Sea
of Galilee (see Matthew 7.9–10). Jesus himself is from a small
peasant village, and the God he shows to the world does not
inhabit any palace but is accessible to all. Nevertheless, the
people are given more than they can eat, so that in all four
versions of the story, the disciples have to gather up twelve
baskets of what is left over at the end.

The crowd arrives with almost nothing. Jesus' first response
to their need in Matthew is to heal their sick, in Mark to give
them teaching, in Luke to do both, but as evening comes his
friends become concerned that the people have had nothing
to eat, and urges Jesus to send them into the villages to buy
food from the local markets, and, in Luke's version, to seek

31

lodging, also. Luke increases the danger for these people, for it is too late for them to get home for the night.

Jesus' response to his friends' concern is to encourage them to go to the markets themselves and buy food for everyone, a suggestion that is patently absurd. When they protest, he asks them to go and see how much food they can find. In a crowd of five thousand, twenty thousand or more, all they can come up with is five loaves and two fish. These people have nothing. Is it because they have rushed to follow Jesus without packing a proper picnic? That is to make a story of heaven mundane. As Mark reminds us, these are people without a shepherd, trapped in a system which ensures their poverty, keeps them away from the centres of power and at the mercy of those who walk their corridors, deprives them of honour and dignity, leaves them at the back of the queue and beyond the edge of the circle. John introduces a profoundly significant detail into his version of the story: he has the disciples find a young boy who has the five loaves and fish with him, and (this is surely what John implies) who offers them to Jesus for his use. In first-century Palestine children had no status, no authority or power – except in Jesus' circle, where, so we are told, he put them in the centre, and declared, 'it is to such as these that the kingdom of God belongs' (Mark 10.14; Matthew 19.14; Luke 18.16). It is entirely appropriate, therefore, that John should put a young boy centre stage, and have his generosity become the means whereby Jesus can lay out God's meal.

Jesus takes the bread and fish, blesses them, and breaks them, and, in John, distributes them, till everyone is fed, till everyone has more than they can eat. John again gets it right. Matthew, Mark and Luke have Jesus give the food to his friends to distribute, no doubt thinking it 'unrealistic' for Jesus himself to hand out the food to such a large crowd. But in symbolic stories of this kind, it does no good to worry about such things. In the story of the Last Supper Jesus will also take, bless, break and distribute (Mark 14.22 and parallels). So let him do it here! Let him act as both host and hostess, doing the work of the father of the family, taking and blessing, as well as the work of the mother, dividing and distributing. Let him be like the father–mother in that stunning Parable of the Two Lost Sons, who runs up the road to greet the younger son, just as a mother would, and who calls the grown-up elder son 'child', just as a mother could. Let him be like that master in Luke 12 who serves his own slaves. Let him portray a God who stands on no ceremony at all, who was content in Bethlehem with a peasant family's hospitality and a manger to lie in, and whose 'throne' will be a cross, and who will bear on his body for all time the marks of crucifixion. Let this remarkable story of the feeding of the crowd take us straight into the heart of the kingdom of God, where the last (and that includes the likes of that young boy) are first, and where those who have nothing receive more than they can cope with. Let this story reveal the extent of God's generosity, and the abundance, the sheer overwhelming plenty to be found always in his presence.

Too often elsewhere the Bible and contemporary preachers present us with a niggardly god who gives to one, but denies another. The father–God of the Parable of the Two Lost Sons embraces both. The feeding of the five thousand is not a ticket-only affair, nor like the Last Supper is it behind closed doors. The men, women and children who are there do not have to prove themselves worthy to receive. The meal happens out in the open, with no boundaries, no walls, no fences, no doors. All the people have to do is turn up, and stretch out their hands to receive. Then the kingdom of God can come, and they can have their daily bread and God's name can be hallowed.

We are so far from the temple in Jerusalem here, and not just geographically. We are in a different world, where people do not need priests or sacrifice to gain access to the mercy of God. And yet this story has let us see right into the Holy of Holies, indeed has taken us inside, so that like Moses and his friends on Sinai, we might behold God and eat and drink. After this there is only one place to go, and that is to the garden of resurrection.

2

The women at the tomb

———◆◆◆———

Mark – Mary of Magdala, Mary the mother of James the younger and of Joses, and Salome

We have a problem with Mark's resurrection story, and it is an insuperable one. His passage runs like this:

> When the Sabbath was over, Mary of Magdala, and Mary the mother of James, and Salome bought spices, so they might go and anoint him. And very early on the first day of the week, just after sunrise, they came to the tomb. They were saying to one another, 'Who will roll away the stone for us from the entrance to the tomb?' when they looked up and saw that the stone had been rolled away (for it was extremely large). Going into the tomb, they saw a young figure sitting on the right-hand side, clothed in a white robe, and they were filled with alarm. But he said to them, 'Do not be alarmed. You are looking for Jesus of Nazareth, the one who was crucified. He is not here. Look, there is the place where they laid him. But go and tell his disciples and Peter that he is going ahead of you to Galilee; there you will see him, just as he told you.' Then they went out and fled from the tomb, for trembling and terror had seized them. And they said nothing to anyone, for they were afraid.   (16.1–8)

And that is all we have, all we have from Mark, at least. A few manuscripts and ancient translations of the text add another verse, and others another 12. They are printed in our Bibles, but everyone agrees Mark did not write them. The single additional verse, known as 'The Shorter Ending', dates from no earlier than the fourth century, and verses 9 to 20, the so-called 'Longer Ending', belong to some time early in the second century, have a style, vocabulary and even theology different from the rest of the Gospel, and are missing from the best of the manuscripts. They amount to little more than a brief, colourless summary of material in the other Gospels, particularly Luke, and also in Acts. The NRSV helpfully puts them in square brackets.

Yet the question remains, did Mark intend to end his Gospel so very abruptly at 16.8? We cannot know the answer to that for certain. It is interesting to see, of course, that at an early stage at least some of the hearers and readers of his Gospel found his ending unsatisfactory, and added verses of their own. Yet we might argue that they did that only to tidy things up, and that in doing so they missed the subtlety of Mark's writing and blunted the edge of its challenge. That, indeed, or something akin to it, has been the argument that has dominated scholarship for some decades now, and still enjoys a large consensus. Some commentators have turned the problematic 16.8 into a masterstroke, and heaped high praise on Mark for his skill. Their attempts, however, have recently been challenged and the debate reopened.

N. T. Wright argues at some length that Mark's original text must have contained further episodes, and that he most probably told of the appearance of the risen Jesus to the women and/or Peter, of the disciples travelling to Galilee and encountering Jesus there, and of Jesus commissioning them to carry on his work of establishing the kingdom of God (*The Resurrection of the Son of God*, pp. 617–24).

N. Clayton Croy devotes a whole book to the question, *The Mutilation of Mark's Gospel* (2004). To be more precise, he devotes a book to the argument that both the beginning and ending of Mark have been lost, and he explains how such losses could have been sustained. On the ending he writes: 'Mark's narrative has been gathering momentum through chapters 14 and 15. It rushes on toward an apex, but then suddenly plunges off the precipice of 16.8' (p. 57). Mark, he argues, has set up his Gospel for a different ending (pp. 57–60). In 16.7 the angel tells the women that Jesus is going ahead of them to Galilee. That is not the first time we hear of that. In 14.28, as Jesus and his disciples are leaving for Gethsemane, where he will be arrested, he says to them, 'After I am raised up, I will go before you to Galilee.' Furthermore, at the end of the transfiguration story Mark has Jesus order his disciples not to tell anyone of it until after he has risen from the dead (9.9). That leads us to expect that his Gospel will include a scene where Jesus is reconciled with his followers and commissions them to continue his work, and will leave us with the expectation that they obey his charge. As Croy says (p. 58), Mark is not in the habit in his Gospel of making predictions and then not reporting their fulfilment. If 16.8 is Mark's intended ending, then he has invented 'a literary genre unparalleled in antiquity: "Gospel Noir"' (p. 53).

N. T. Wright is undoubtedly correct to sound a note of caution: 'If it is at least a serious possibility that Mark really did have a fuller ending which is now lost, it is simply unsafe to proceed as though *ephobounto gar*' (the 'for they were afraid' of 16.8) 'were his final word to the waiting world' (*The Resurrection of the Son of God*, p. 617).

So we will have to comment on 16.1–8 knowing that it may well be a damaged text. We will not make anything of its abrupt ending, because Mark might not have intended it. There might be a page missing – Croy suggests in his chapter 7 that we should think of the autograph copy being a codex, an early kind of book, rather than a scroll. At the same time, we will not try to tidy things up, as the writers of the Shorter and Longer Ending attempted to do, nor will we speculate any further about what Mark might have written. We will have to be content with what we know comes from his hand. We will have to conclude our discussion with '. . .' and then move on to the other three Gospels, which all take the story further.

We have heard of two of these women in Mark, probably all three, before. Mary of Magdala and Salome are among the women who look on from a distance as Jesus is crucified (15.40). That group also includes a 'Mary the mother of James the younger' (or 'James the little') 'and Joses'. Presumably she is the same woman as 'Mary the mother of James' in 16.1, and we are encouraged to think so by the verse immediately preceding, which speaks of Mary of Magdala and 'Mary the mother of Joses' being witnesses to Jesus' burial. It seems clear that Mark is using shorthand in the second and third cases, only referring to one of that Mary's sons instead of both.

All four Gospels tell of women at the cross, at the burial and at the empty tomb. Mark and Matthew speak *only* of women, except for Joseph of Arimathea who performs the burial. John does not make explicit mention of any of the women witnessing the burial scene, but in the very next passage he has Mary of Magdala going to the tomb while it is still dark, knowing exactly where to go and which tomb to make for. So he too invites us to imagine that at least that Mary is present when Jesus is buried.

Luke and John both also place male disciples at the crucifixion, and John brings two to the empty tomb. Famously, John has the 'disciple whom Jesus loved' near the cross (19.26), and that same male disciple, along with Peter, will discover the empty tomb (20.3–10). Luke, intriguingly, talks in his story of the crucifixion of 'all Jesus' acquaintances and the women who had come with him from Galilee' looking on from a distance (23.49). Who those other 'acquaintances' were, he does not say. Whether we are meant to think of them including Peter and the other members of the Twelve (apart from Judas Iscariot, Jesus' betrayer), we cannot tell. In his story of Jesus' arrest, which is generally close to the versions in Mark and Matthew, he does not speak of those male disciples fleeing from the scene (compare the end of his account in 22.53 with Mark 14.52 or Matthew 26.56). On the other hand, when Jesus is dragged off for trial, Luke follows Mark and Matthew in telling of Peter, and only Peter, going along at a safe distance, to see what happens. And then, of course, Peter denies Jesus and, like the others among the Twelve, disappears from the scene. Whoever the 'acquaintances' are at the cross, Luke makes it hard for us to imagine Peter or any of the Twelve among them, though the Greek term he uses shows they do include men.

Luke further departs from Matthew and John in not having women and only women as the first to meet the risen Jesus.

He accords that privilege to a male disciple called Cleopas and to his unnamed companion. It is perfectly possible for us to think of that companion as a woman, indeed, the most natural interpretation is that she is his wife, but we cannot be sure.

Though the accounts vary, the Gospels contain enough to suggest that in the early Church it was a group of women who first took the lead in speaking of the crucifixion, the burial and the resurrection. Their testimony was crucial. Though some spoke of some male disciples being involved at various points, no one, it seems, had any doubt that women were there as Jesus died and was buried, and that they were the first to stumble upon the resurrection. Even John, who has Peter and the beloved disciple run to the tomb, tells of how Mary of Magdala sets them running. It is she who first discovers the empty tomb, and who in a panic rushes back to tell Peter and the other disciple (John 20.1–2). But for her, they would remain in their beds. And though they then find the tomb for themselves, and though the beloved disciple 'sees and believes' (see 20.8), it is Mary, and Mary alone, who stays behind and meets the risen Christ.

The names of the women at the cross, the burial and the empty tomb are not the same in all four Gospels, except for one.

Matthew omits Salome from his lists, and instead has Mary of Magdala, together with Mary the mother of James and Joseph and the unnamed mother of the sons of Zebedee, at the cross, and Mary of Magdala and 'the other Mary' (presumably more shorthand for Mary, James and Joseph's mother) at the burial and the empty tomb.

Luke does not supply any names for the women at the crucifixion and the burial; they are simply 'the women who had come with him from Galilee'. He does, however, give the names of Mary of Magdala, Joanna and Mary the mother of James in the story of the empty tomb. Back in 8.1–3 he makes all too brief mention of women who become Jesus' disciples in Galilee, Mary of Magdala, Joanna, Susanna and 'many others'. Clearly we must presume that when he speaks of 'the women who had followed him from Galilee' being there at the crucifixion and the burial, we must include the two Marys of his resurrection scene and Joanna among them.

John, as everyone knows, has Mary, Jesus' own mother, as well as Mary of Magdala at the cross. He has another woman there, too, though she is too often forgotten: another Mary, the sister of Jesus' mother and wife of Clopas (19.25). We have already seen that he implies that Mary of Magdala is a witness of the burial as well, and she goes first to the tomb with another unnamed woman or other women, though they lie deep in the shadows of John's narrative and are only glimpsed in a single verb. When she returns to the tomb, Mary of Magdala is on her own. It is often John's habit to clear the stage of everyone except Jesus and one other person. Think, for example, of the story in his chapter 4 of the meeting between Jesus and the Samaritan woman.

No doubt John believed his technique made for more powerful drama. He was right. The long story of the Samaritan woman is a stunning piece, and the story of Mary of Magdala encountering the risen Jesus in John 20 is so striking and so memorable that the other women from the resurrection stories in the other Gospels too have been cast into its shadows, where often they have been left ignored. Admittedly, the witness of the other three Gospels encourages us to single Mary of Magdala out from the others, for she is the only one to be there in all of them, in all three scenes.

As we explore the resurrection stories let us remember Mary the mother of James and Joses or Joseph, Salome, Joanna and 'the other women', as well as Mary of Magdala. And let us not presume that just because none are mentioned in the book of Acts, they did not play a vital role in the spread of the early Church, and that their job was done once they had brought the news of the resurrection to the male disciples. Acts does not tell the whole story – as if any one account could – and Luke has chosen to focus our attention on male leaders, Peter, Stephen for a spell, and then Paul. Just as John's portrayal of Mary of Magdala tempts us to forget the other women of the resurrection, so Luke succeeds in putting them out of our minds entirely. That is a tragedy, and the Church has been grievously wounded as a result. Even now, in my own Church of England, there are some who do not recognize the status of women ordained priest and, though significant progress has been made towards their eventual consecration, we still have no women bishops. How different things might have been and might be now, if Luke had devoted (shall we say?) seven chapters of Acts to Mary of Magdala, three to Mary the mother of James, and three to Joanna, the third member of his named trio!

But let us return to Mark and his story.

The women act as quickly as they can. They go out to the shops as soon as they are open on the Saturday evening, after the Sabbath, and buy spices to anoint Jesus' body. Does that mean Joseph has not had time to anoint him for the burial? It would seem so. Mark only mentions Joseph buying a linen shroud, lifting Jesus' body down from the cross, wrapping it in the shroud, and then laying it in the tomb and rolling the stone across the entrance (15.46). It seems the burial has not been done properly. Joseph has either been negligent or, much more likely, in too much of a hurry. Mark has Jesus die at three in the afternoon. By the time Joseph has secured Pilate's permission to bury the body, it is already evening (see 15.42), and the Sabbath has already begun, or is just about to.

The women have followed Jesus all the way from Galilee. We would not have guessed that from any of the Gospels, if Luke had not introduced us to three of them in 8.1–3, and if Mark, Matthew and again Luke had not mentioned it in their accounts of the crucifixion. Such women were not just camp followers. We must not be misled by Luke's telling us that Mary of Magdala, Joanna and Susanna used to support Jesus and his other followers out of their own resources (8.3), as if that was all they did. His story two chapters later, at 10.38–42, of Jesus' visit to the home of the sisters Martha and Mary, is most revealing. Mary sits at Jesus' feet and listens to him, while Martha busies herself with domestic tasks. Martha is only doing what would normally be expected of her, and her protest that her sister is leaving her to do all the work is, by the conventions of the times, perfectly understandable. Yet Martha is not just claiming that Mary's behaviour is unfair. She is implying it is not proper for a woman to be a disciple

– for sitting at Jesus' feet and listening to his teaching is precisely what his disciples do. Martha's contemporaries, and Luke's also, of course, would have expected Jesus to take Martha's side, and to send Mary off to do the 'women's' work. But he does not. 'Mary has chosen the better part,' he tells Martha. It is an astonishing statement, and challenges the prevailing beliefs about the roles of men and women at a fundamental level.

Thank God Luke tells this story in his Gospel! And how very sad that he did not write everything in the rest of his Gospel in the light of it, and that the other three evangelists so often leave us with the impression that Jesus was surrounded by exclusively male disciples, and that only men belonged to his inner circle. There are far too few stories about his women followers. Yet it is partly our fault. Too often we assume that when the Gospel writers mention 'disciples', without giving us any further details, they only have men in mind, perhaps only the Twelve. At least the resurrection stories, together with those of the crucifixion and burial, clearly call that assumption into question.

So the three *disciples*, Mary of Magdala, Mary the mother of James and Joses, and Salome, get up very early on the Sunday morning, at first light, to go to the tomb. They arrive too late, or so we might think. Mary of Magdala will go to the tomb even earlier in John, while it is still dark, but she will be 'too late', also. By the time she reaches the tomb, Jesus will not be there. In all the Gospels the women miss the resurrection itself. Of course they do. As we have already remarked, the resurrection of Jesus takes us deep into the heart of the mystery of God. It cannot be pinned down. Let us suppose for a moment the women get there sooner, with modern wristwatches hidden beneath the edges of their sleeves. Will they be able to note the exact time it 'happens'? Even to ask the question is to step out of the circle of the divine into the mundane, and to arrive in a very different kind of story.

In the second half of the second century someone wrote what is called the Gospel of Peter. It bears Peter's name and claims to have been written by him, but it has nothing to do with him. It is far too late and parts of it are nastily anti-

Semitic, too. Only a fragment has survived, and it is entirely taken up with the crucifixion and resurrection. It contains this passage:

> Now in the night in which the Lord's day dawned, when the soldiers were keeping guard, two by two in each watch, there was a loud voice in heaven, and they saw the heavens open and two men come down from there in a great brightness and draw near to the sepulchre. That stone which had been laid against the entrance to the sepulchre started of itself to roll and move sidewards, and the sepulchre was opened and both men entered.
>
> When those soldiers saw this, they awakened the centurion and the elders, for they also were there to mount guard. And while they were narrating what they had seen, they saw three men come out from the sepulchre, two of them supporting the other and a cross following them and the heads of the two reaching to heaven, but that of him who was being led reached beyond the heavens.
>
> (9.35—10.40, J. K. Elliott's edition of
The Apocryphal New Testament, 1993, p. 156)

It is useful to have that passage with which to compare the Gospel stories. When we come to Matthew, we will pose the question whether he slips from drama into melodrama, but even then the Gospel of Peter will reveal how restrained Matthew's account is, and how much room it leaves for mystery. The Gospel of Peter leaves very little. Curiously enough, its account works best at the beginning and the very end, for there we find ourselves in a strange and wonderful land that might seem to befit resurrection. But the overall effect is ruined by the rest. The writer tries to describe what cannot be described, what Mark, Matthew, Luke and John all knew could not be described and so left wrapped in silence. We have already said that it only takes a phrase, a few words to slip from the sublime into the ridiculous. As soon as the Gospel of Peter begins talking of the stone rolling to the side, it has descended into the ridiculous, and the description of Jesus emerging from the tomb is pure bathos. Mark, Matthew, Luke and John leave that alone. None attempts to take us to the resurrection itself, but only to its aftermath. They let God be God, and that is why they have their place in our Bibles, and the Gospel of Peter mercifully does not.

So the women in Mark do not encounter the resurrection. Resurrection, of course, is not what they have come for. They have come for the marking of death. They have come for the wrong reasons, for when they reach the tomb they find that death has been undone. In any case they need not have bought their expensive spices for, so Mark has told us, an unnamed woman, in the Bethany house of a leper called Simon, has already broken a 'jar of very costly perfume, genuine nard' and poured it all over his head, and Jesus has declared that she has anointed his body for burial (14.3–9).

On their way to the tomb, they worry about how they are to shift the stone from the entrance to the tomb. We have to think of a tomb not sunk into the ground, but cut horizontally into rock, with a shelf or trough for the body inside, and a large round stone set in a groove and rolled across the entrance. We might suggest, if we felt sufficiently churlish, that the women should have thought about the stone before they set out. Yet does not the late timing of their concern only emphasize their grief, and the depth of both their loyalty to Jesus and their concern to complete his burial? Grief, particularly after the horrors of crucifixion, cannot allow any of them to think straight, while their quickly purchasing the spices and setting off at dawn the next day only emphasizes their remarkable determination – the stone presents a problem, but they will cross that bridge when they come to it. Standing on the commanding height of the resurrection, we must not condemn the women for their foolishness.

We have also to recognize that Jesus' resurrection is beyond all their expectations. Five times in Mark's Gospel, Jesus explicitly predicts his resurrection. In 9.9 only Peter, James and John are present, in 10.32–34 he takes the Twelve aside, and in 14.28 he is speaking again just with the Twelve. But in 8.31 and 9.31 he is on the road with 'his disciples' and there is no mention of his teaching an inner circle. As we learn when we reach the crucifixion, the women are among those travelling with him. We have every reason to imagine them hearing what he has to say. Yet no doubt the brutality of the crucifixion and the terrible events preceding it have knocked all that out of them, and not just them, either. The other three Gospels all present other disciples, including men, finding the news of the resurrection very hard to come to terms with. There was, after all, no precedent for it. Those who meet the risen Christ find themselves suddenly confronted with a God who has been through a brutal death, and bears its marks upon him. No such story had ever been told before.

The women in Mark do not, of course, get that far, not at least within the confines of 16.1–8, but still they find themselves on the brink of such an encounter. The 'young figure' inside the tomb, that belongs to God's world and comes with its wisdom, tells them so. 'You are looking for Jesus of Nazareth, the one who was crucified,' the angel says. 'He is not here.' They are looking for the man they have followed from Galilee, the one they saw fighting for breath on a Roman gibbet, the one who cried, 'My God, my God, why have you abandoned me?' and then died – or rather, they have come for his corpse. But they can no more have the familiar Jesus back, the Jesus they thought they knew, than they can anoint his cold, already decomposing body. They have come for their friend, their teacher, their healer, lying prone on the cold rock, and they have stumbled upon heaven. They have come for death, and they have found life. They have come for the silence of the tomb, and they have heard the voice of an angel. They have come to hide the stench of death beneath the odours of their spices, but there is now no need for them to break their jars, as that other woman did in Simon's house.

All else is mystery and is enough to send them running away in fear. But not before they have been given a new job to do. Their spice jars may be useless, but they have a task to perform which is hugely more important. They are to tell the other disciples of what they have found. They are to say they must all return to Galilee and there they will 'see' Jesus. It is like saying they will 'see' God, exactly like saying they will see God. And of course they are to share in the encounter: 'There *you* will see him,' the angel says.

Do these three women meet Jesus on the way? They do in Matthew, but Mark ends before any encounter takes place. It ends with '. . .' There is nothing else we can say, no use in speculation. Mark 16.1–8 has brought us to the edge of resurrection. The final words, 'for they were afraid' are left hanging in the air. Yet, most decidedly, it is not the fetid air of death.

Matthew – Mary of Magdala, and Mary the mother of James and Joseph

Let us begin, not with Matthew's text, but with R. S. Thomas' poem 'Alive'.

> It is alive. It is you,
> God. Looking out I can see
> no death. The earth moves, the
> sea moves, the wind goes
> on its exuberant
> journeys. Many creatures
> reflect you, the flowers
> your colour, the tides the precision
> of your calculations. There
> is nothing too ample
> for you to overflow, nothing
> so small that your workmanship
> is not revealed. I listen
> and it is you speaking.
> I find the place where you lay
> warm. At night, if I waken,
> there are the sleepless conurbations
> of the stars. The darkness
> is the deepening shadow
> of your presence; the silence a
> process in the metabolism
> of the being of love.

And now to Matthew:

> After the Sabbath, as the first day of the week was dawning, Mary of Magdala and the other Mary went to see

45

the tomb. And behold, there was a great earthquake! For an angel of the Lord, descending from heaven, came and rolled away the stone and sat on it. His appearance was like lightning and his clothing white as snow. The guards quaked with fear of him and became as dead men. But the angel answered and said to the women, 'You must not be afraid, for I know that you are looking for Jesus, the one who was crucified. He is not here, for he has been raised, as he said he would be. Come, see the place where he lay. Then quick, go and tell his disciples, "He has been raised from the dead, and behold he is going ahead of you to Galilee; there you will see him." See I have told you!'

They quickly left the tomb with fear and great joy, and ran to tell his disciples the news. And behold, Jesus met them, and said, 'Greetings!' They came forward, grasped his feet and worshipped him. Then Jesus said to them, 'Do not be afraid. Go and tell my brothers the news, so that they go to Galilee; there they will see me.'

(28.1–10)

R. S. Thomas is much quieter than Matthew. We can hear the silence in his poem, while Matthew is all hustle and bustle. His story is a noisier one than Mark's, too. It has an earthquake for starters, matching the one that takes place in his crucifixion scene, at the point when Jesus dies. Mark and Luke are content at that point to speak of the veil of the temple being torn in two, and for John there is no need of any such miracle at all, because for him the triumph of God in the death of Jesus is enough. But Matthew has the earth shaking, rocks splitting and even tombs opening, 'the saints' emerging and entering Jerusalem, and many people seeing them (27.51–53). All this, and the earthquake at the empty tomb, with the angel descending from heaven, rolling back the stone and sitting on it, might seem pure Hollywood. Certainly, it is a very different way of speaking from Mark's, or from Luke or John's for that matter.

Yet we should not be too quick to dismiss it as sheer sensationalism, the needless embroidery of a good tale. Take the seemingly bizarre example of the opening of the tombs at Jesus' death and the entry of the dead into Jerusalem. Such language, like that of the calming of a storm, of a walking on the sea, or the turning of five loaves and two fish into more than enough food for twenty thousand people, is not to be taken literally. It is metaphor, and it is what it signifies that matters. In the case of the dead rising from their tombs, it signals the start of the general resurrection of the dead! That is a remarkable claim on Matthew's part. To use the colourful phrase of John Dominic Crossan, it means 'the Great Divine Clean-Up' (*The Resurrection of Jesus: The Crossan–Wright Dialogue*, pp. 24–5) is underway, and that the iron grip of death, especially the violent death of faithful martyrs (the saints), has been broken. Crossan says (p. 25), 'The end of the world is not what we are talking about. We're talking about cosmic transformation of this world from a world of evil and injustice and impurity and violence into a world of justice and peace and purity and holiness.' Central to Jesus' own teaching, he continues, was the claim that this cosmic transformation had already started. The kingdom of God, or the kingdom of heaven, as Matthew prefers to call it, did not just belong to the future, even to the years soon to come, but was already present, already overlapping the world of Rome and the Herods, and Jesus' followers were called with him to make it happen.

So when Matthew speaks of earthquake, the dead bursting from their tombs, an angel descending to a tomb and rolling away the entrance stone with his little finger (I cannot stop myself adding a little more drama still), he is trying to underline the momentous character of the events. They are truly of cosmic significance, and just as Jesus' birth in Matthew's Gospel is marked by the movement of a star, so Jesus' death and resurrection are accompanied by a movement of the earth.

Yet the women at the tomb seem at first to be somewhat diminished in the process, dwarfed by all the razzmatazz. There are only two of them for a start, and they have nothing to say in this whole passage. At least in Mark we overhear them talking on their way to the tomb. And Matthew has a different reason for their going, also. They have not rushed out on the Saturday to buy their spices or, if they have, Matthew does not mention it. They go to 'see the tomb'. That is not an unworthy aim, of course. Their purpose may be to make final devotions at the tomb, in accordance with the customs of their time. But it might seem they have not gone to so much trouble to prepare for these devotions as the women in Mark, and are not going to bear the cost of the highly unpleasant task of anointing a body which has already had time to start decomposing.

Furthermore, when the angel gives them their orders, it seems he does not count them among the disciples. Instead they are to break the news 'to the disciples', and then, it would seem, bow out of the action. 'He has been raised from the dead,' they are to say to the disciples, 'and behold he is going ahead of *you* to Galilee; there *you* will see him.' They are not charged to say, 'He is going ahead of *us* to Galilee; there *we* will see him.' If the angel is to be trusted, it would seem they are meant to stay behind in Jerusalem, and will not see the risen Jesus with the others. They are merely to be the messenger-girls, and are not invited to the party. The contrast with Mark might seem small, but at this stage it seems devastating. For Mark has the angel say to the women, 'He is going ahead of you to Galilee; there you will see him.' Those women will not be excluded. They have their place securely within the circle of the disciples.

As it turns out, however, Matthew's angel is not as well informed as Mark's or, to put it another way, Jesus himself will ignore the angel's bias: he will meet the women on the way, and they, not the men, will be the first to find him. After what the angel has said, that encounter comes as a complete surprise, not just to the women, but to us, the readers of the story and, no doubt, to the angel, too. Do we detect a playfulness in Matthew's writing and the way he handles the plot in this scene? Some commentators find muddle. I am not so sure.

But we have jumped too far ahead. Let us return to the beginning. Matthew does not at first clarify the women's motive for going to the tomb, beyond their going to 'see' it.

Warren Carter argues they come in the light of Jesus' predictions of his rising to await the resurrection (*Matthew and the Margins: A Socio-Political and Religious Reading*, 2000, p. 544; see also p. 539 on 27.61). I cannot be so confident as that. Matthew has retained too much ambiguity, and not said enough. Yet at least the women *go*. None of the men do. None of the other disciples, those the angel seems to regard as the proper disciples, are there. At this key moment in the story, *the* key moment in the story, only two women are present, and we have heard nothing of them before, apart from the fact that they have followed Jesus all the way from Galilee, and have witnessed his death and burial. They have been mentioned twice before, but this is the first (and only) story where they are centre or near-centre stage. No doubt, historically it was not their last. No doubt, as we have already suggested, they played a crucial role in the formation and care of the infant Church, and that is why this story was told and retold about them.

And there is more to their going to the tomb than at first Matthew allows to meet our eye. The angel will reveal to us that they have gone not for the tomb, but for Jesus, 'the one who was crucified'. Somehow, in a way Matthew does not specify, they will try to reply to the mockery they heard surrounding the cross with the new sounds of their grief and their devotions; whether or not they carry spices with them (for we must not argue too much from Matthew's silence; ultimately he leaves the matter open), they mean to respond to the brutality of that death with their care and love. The men were in charge on Golgotha, the centurion and his soldiers, the chief priests, scribes and elders. Well, now it is the turn of the women. They will take over and do what they can.

Only it does not happen like that, of course, for things at the tomb are not what they expect. Because of Matthew's histrionics, they see more at the tomb than any others in any of the other Gospels. They arrive just as the earth begins to shake and as the angel descends from heaven. They see him roll away the stone and then sit on it. But they still do not see the risen Jesus emerging from the tomb. This is the Gospel of Matthew, not the Gospel of Peter. They do not find resurrection.

49

They find *nothing*! They are looking for a mutilated, dead body. And that is gone. They are looking for Jesus, and he is not there. They find nothing . . . except an angel.

And they see him sitting on the entrance stone! At this point I find myself wanting to tap Matthew on the shoulder and say, 'Better omit that bit. Too down-to-earth. By all means have an angel descending from heaven. That is clear metaphor. But sitting on a stone, that won't do. You're bringing heaven down to earth, fine, wonderful, but you mustn't turn heaven *into* earth!'

The tomb by itself is simply bewildering, terrifying. Sometimes Christians talk as if belief in the empty tomb lies at the heart of the faith. The Gospels do not share that view. As Matthew makes plain, the tomb is nothing without the angel. Of itself it proves nothing, it achieves nothing. It is the angel who takes the women into the divine, and of course they will go much deeper into God's territory when they meet Jesus on the road.

And we are not talking just of profound religious experience here, though surely we are speaking of that, but of a divine call to action. As in Mark, the angel gives the women a job to do, and the risen Jesus reminds them of it. For them the resurrection is not the end, but a new beginning, and one of even greater significance than the one they had in Galilee, when first they met him. For now they know where they are, and who it is they have been keeping company all this time.

Matthew has had no angels appear in his Gospel since the start of his story, when three times one appears to Joseph in a dream (1.20; 2.13, 19), and angels wait on Jesus after his temptation in the wilderness (4.11). There has been plenty of talk of angels, however. 'For the Son of Man is to come with his angels in the glory of his Father,' Jesus has said (16.27). Well now the time has arrived, or very nearly. The Great Divine Clean-Up has begun!

Matthew's Gospel thus sits between an angel's wings, as the ark of the covenant in the Holy of Holies in the temple once sat between the wings of the cherubim. And there are other respects in which the end of his Gospel reminds us of its beginning. The women leave the tomb with fear, as they do in Mark, but also with 'great joy'. Then, when they meet Jesus on the road they grasp his feet and worship him. When the magi see the star over the house where Jesus is born, they too are overcome with 'great joy', and when they go inside and find the child, they 'fall on their knees and worship him' (2.10–11).

Like the magi, the women are to some extent outsiders. Though they have followed Jesus all the way from Galilee, and remained with him through thick and thin, stayed close when others have fled the scene, yet we have heard next to nothing about them. Luke tells us Mary of Magdala was healed by Jesus (8.2). Matthew does not tell us that. All this time the women have been in the wings of his story, invisible. Until the crucifixion, we did not even know they were there. And the angel does not regard them as disciples, either. As for the magi, they come from the east, where (so people said then) too much superstitious nonsense comes from. They belong to a world that often accused magi of helping to perpetrate that nonsense. Like the women at the tomb, they go to the wrong place at first. The women go to the tomb, when they need to be in Galilee; the magi go first to Jerusalem, expecting to find the new 'king of the Jews' in the heart of the political and religious establishment. The women expect to find a corpse and meet a God; the magi travel expecting a king at the end of their long journey entirely different from the one they meet in Bethlehem.

The magi fall on their knees and worship the newborn Jesus. Is that why Matthew portrays the women grasping the feet of the risen Jesus when they worship him? Does he put it that way, so we can more easily compare these two women to the magi, and wonder at things coming full circle? His description of the magi worshipping the child is wholly appropriate. But is it equally appropriate to speak of the women 'grasping the feet' of the risen Christ? Is this another detail, like the angel sitting on the stone, where we have to tap Matthew on the shoulder, or get out our red pen? Perhaps it is, but there is more to say. For we have already argued that such physical language used of God or the divine can function as the language of intimacy. If that is the case here, then the women come closer to God than the magi in Bethlehem. For the magi do not touch Jesus, but only kneel before him. The women 'touch', even 'grasp' the risen Jesus. I would immediately understand such terms as metaphor, just as 'seeing' or 'hearing' God is metaphor. Whether it is powerful metaphor, or beyond the mark, is for each one of us to decide. Taking it out of the world of theological and historical debate, and into prayer, we might find that 'touching God', or 'touching the risen Jesus' does indeed evoke a sense of God's intimacy in a most extraordinary way, but that 'grasping his feet' destroys it. If it were left to me, I think I might get out my red pen and make a small alteration.

We began this section not with Matthew, but with the poet R. S. Thomas. It is good to have such poets around, for they remind us we must always approach the writers of the Gospels, whenever they speak of God, as dealers in poetic speech. And here it is very good to have that particular poem 'Alive', for it becomes a gentle commentary on Matthew's passage, and in particular that marvellous line and a bit, 'I find the place where you lay warm.'

The women expect to come to the place where Jesus lies cold, but instead they do indeed find the place where he lay warm. He is no longer there. The tomb could not hold him, for what can hold God? Not the universe, for sure, nor the Holy of Holies, nor any religion, church or doctrine. So often, as we make our own journey through the world, the best we can hope for is to come across 'the place where he lay warm'.

Yet sometimes it seems we do more than that. Certainly it is not the whole story for the two women. They 'meet' Jesus, or rather Jesus 'meets' them. They 'hear' him. They 'touch' him. They 'touch' God. They are commissioned, given a new task, a new purpose. They will never be the same again.

Alas, the soldiers at the tomb will not be changed, not if the chief priests from whom they receive their orders have their way. Matthew is the only Gospel writer who has Jesus' tomb guarded, and his purpose is clear. When Jesus is buried, the chief priests and Pharisees recall, so he tells us, that he has said he will rise from the dead. Just in case the disciples steal the body and then put it around that he has indeed been raised, they go to Pilate and ask for some Roman soldiers to mount guard on the tomb. Pilate tells them to use their own temple police (Matthew 27.62–66). And so it is, that when the women arrive at the tomb, they are not alone, and they are not the only ones to see the angel, either.

But the soldiers do not see what the women see, nor hear what they hear. They do not run away to Galilee in great joy, either, but go back to the chief priests. There they tell them everything that has happened, but what is that, we wonder? Surely their report will be very different from the one the women will give the disciples in Galilee. Whatever it is, the chief priests and the elders they consult remain firmly entrenched in the world of power politics and deceit in which Matthew has located them. They give the soldiers a hefty bribe, and tell them to say, 'His disciples came by night and stole him when we were asleep'! That, of course, sounds like dereliction of duty. But not to worry: if Pilate gets to hear of it, they will sort him out, and make sure the soldiers do not take the rap (28.11–15).

Matthew suggests, and we have no reason to doubt him, that the soldiers' tale about the disciples stealing the body was still doing the rounds in his own day, and was being used against the Christian communities. He is trying here to explain how it came to be invented. Whether we believe his account, and think it was based on real inside information, or whether we suppose that he or one of his Christian sources has made it up to answer their critics, is up to us. It is certainly coloured by the extreme hostility towards the Jewish religious author-ities that we come across so often in the Gospels, and is the more suspicious as a result.

Yet whatever we think about its historicity, its importance is larger than we might imagine. We said earlier that the tomb is nothing without the angel. The story of the soldiers reminds us that even *with* the angel it is not necessarily enough. The women, we might say, are brought to life by him, but he renders the soldiers like 'dead men'. The women have come to the tomb expecting to find a corpse; now they seem to have several on their hands! Clearly much depends on how the experience of the angel is received, though ultimately what makes the difference for the women is their meeting with the risen Jesus.

And that both brings us back to the heart of the matter, and also leaves us wondering whether Matthew's story does not contain a flaw more serious than the little ones we have suggested already. He does not really tell us what the deeper impact on the soldiers might have been. He simply presents them as men who obey orders. 'So they took the money and did as they were told,' is his final word on them (28.15a). Admittedly, the Jewish religious authorities are the true villains of his piece, but Matthew seems to leave the soldiers trapped in their dark, duplicitous, self-seeking world. He seems to leave them beyond the bounds of redemption, so that we cannot possibly imagine the risen Jesus meeting *them*. And if we cannot imagine that of the soldiers, whose inner world is concealed from us, then what hope can we possibly conceive for the Jewish authorities? They would seem to be left entirely outside the sphere of God's mercy, destined for 'the eternal fire prepared for the devil and his angels', of which Matthew speaks in his Parable of the Judgement of the Gentiles (24.31–46, especially verse 41).

Yet surely that cannot be right. For no one belongs beyond the reach of the prodigal generosity of God. We make his mercy and love far too small if we imagine that anyone does. Even when we are exploring a story as fine as this one of Matthew's, we must keep our wits about us, and keep asking questions.

Luke – Mary of Magdala, Joanna, Mary the mother of James, and the other women

When we picture the scene of the empty tomb to ourselves, how many women must we put on stage? Mark has three, Matthew two, and John only one, though he suggests at one point that Mary of Magdala goes first to the tomb with one or more companions. Luke gives the names of three, Mary of Magdala, Joanna and Mary the mother of James. The two Marys we have already found in Mark and Matthew, but Joanna appears only in Luke's Gospel: here, by implication at the crucifixion and burial, and in 8.1–3, where we find this:

Soon afterwards Jesus went on through towns and villages, preaching and bringing the good news of the kingdom of God. The Twelve were with him, and some women who had been cured of evil spirits and infirmities: Mary called Magdalene, from whom seven demons had gone out, and Joanna, the wife of Chuza, Herod's steward, Susanna, and many other women who provided for them out of their own resources.

It might seem that the information about Joanna is pretty sparse, but it is enough for Richard Bauckham in his book *Gospel Women* (2002) to devote 94 pages to her. The identification of her as married to one of the most powerful officials in the court of Herod Antipas in Tiberias enables him to reconstruct her setting:

As Chuza's wife Joanna lived in a magnificent house in the new city of Tiberias [on the shores of the Sea of Galilee] with estates elsewhere in Galilee. She became part of the would-be romanized culture of the Tiberian aristocracy and court officials, who aped the life and manners of the Roman aristocracy . . . Wealth was conspicuous, and the political maneuvering and sycophancy of the court were inescapable.   (p. 195)

Her social position put her at a distance from the vast majority of people, and her being married to Chuza and being part of Herod's court would have marked her for many Jews as a traitor to their national and religious cause. Like Mary from Magdala, a town further up the western shore of the Sea of Galilee, Susanna and the others, she seems first to have encountered Jesus when she went to him for healing. From then on her life changed utterly. She was restored to health, but that was only the beginning. She became a disciple, and with the other women joined Jesus as he went from town to town, and village to village, and remained with him on his journey to Jerusalem. Bauckham again:

Throwing in her lot with Jesus was a radical conversion to the poor, but it must have been the nondiscriminating acceptance with which the community of Jesus' disciples welcomed all who joined them, even tax collectors, that gave her the confidence to risk her reputation among her peers, burning her bridges behind her, in order to identify herself as fully as possible with Jesus and his movement. Among these people her status brought her no honor; not even her substantial donations to the common fund gave her a place above others. But instead she found a place in what Jesus called his new family of those who were practicing the will of God.   (p. 196)

And here she is, clutching her jar of spices in her hand, hurrying with her friends to Jesus' tomb in the light of a new dawn:

The women rested on the Sabbath in obedience to the commandment. But on the first day of the week at the crack of dawn they came to the tomb, bringing the spices they had prepared. They found the stone rolled back from the tomb, and going inside they failed to find the body of the Lord Jesus. While they were perplexed about this, suddenly two men in dazzling robes stood beside them. Terrified, they bowed their faces to the ground. The men said to them, 'Why do you seek the living among the dead? He is not here, but risen. Remember what he told you, when he was still in Galilee: "The Son of Man must be handed over into the hands of sinful men and be crucified, and on the third day rise again."' Then they did remember his words. Returning from the tomb, they reported all this to the Eleven and to all the others.

Now the women were Mary of Magdala and Joanna and Mary the mother of James; there were other women with them, too. They kept telling the apostles these things, but their stories seemed to them so much nonsense, and they did not believe them. But Peter got up and ran to the tomb. He peered inside, and saw only the linen wrappings. He went away wondering what had happened.   (Luke 23.56b—24.12)

Luke has firmly put his own stamp on the empty tomb story. We asked a moment ago how many women we should imagine at the tomb. Luke leaves the matter open. While only three are named, he speaks of other women being there, too. We seem to have small crowd here. He gives the same motive for going as Mark: they go to anoint Jesus' body. They go to find a corpse and to complete a burial done in haste when already 'the Sabbath was beginning' (23.54). They do not worry about how they will manage to shift the stone, but they are utterly bewildered by what they find when they get there. The empty tomb by itself only increases their sense of loss. John will dwell on that point, when he comes to his story of Mary of Magdala.

In Mark the women were met by 'a young figure', and in Matthew by 'an angel of the Lord'. Here the women are met by 'two men'. But we should not be deceived by that word 'men'. When three 'men' visit Abraham while he is taking his siesta (Genesis 18.2), they are in truth God himself and two companions from heaven. On that occasion the three figures are remarkably well disguised, and Abraham never seems to realize who they are. But in this case the clothes the figures are wearing give them away. Later on in Luke 24, at verse 23, this encounter will be described as 'a vision of angels'. The women immediately know where they are. They are in the presence of the divine, and so they bow their faces to the ground in terror. We would expect the angels to tell them not to be afraid. That is the usual biblical response of God or his angels to those who are frightened by their appearing. It is so in Mark 16.6 and in Matthew 28.5, and at the beginning of the Gospel of Luke itself, when an angel appears to Zechariah, or Mary of Nazareth, or the shepherds – his first words in each case are, 'Do not be afraid' (1.13, 30; 2.10). Not so here. Instead of reassurance, the angels pose a question and administer a gentle rebuke. The women should have known. Did not Jesus tell them? Yes he did, back in 9.22: 'The Son of Man must suffer many things, be rejected by the elders, chief priests and scribes, and be put to death, and on the third day be raised.' These words are said by Jesus to 'the disciples', and by this time Mary of Magdala, Joanna and the others have joined their company.

Yet the rebuke might still seem a bit harsh, as if on entering the tomb the women should have cried, 'Oh, of course! Silly us! He's been raised from the dead, just like he said. Should have known.' But if the reality of death is never what we expect, if when someone we love dies, even after a long illness, it is never quite as we thought it would be, then how much more will resurrection be beyond all expectation, when there is no precedent for it, no prior experience from which to learn? And for God's sake, the women have just seen their friend crucified and accompanied his body to its hurried burial!

But the angels are right, of course. By the terms of Luke's story, the women should have known. They should not have come to the tomb with spices in their hands to anoint a corpse. They should not have come to the tomb at all, for it is now a glorious irrelevance. 'Why do you seek the living among the dead?' Why indeed.

The disciples in Luke, including the Twelve when they have been told about it on their own, never have understood Jesus' predictions of his death and resurrection (see 9.43b–45; 18.33–34). At least from this point on, once the angels have reminded the women of Jesus' words, their reactions are exemplary. Yes, they *do* remember! And they go straight back to the Eleven and the others and tell them everything. Mark 16.8 says the women flee in terror and say nothing to anyone. We doubt that was the end of it in Mark's original copy, but it is all we have got. Matthew does not speak directly of the women reporting back to the others (despite their having considerably more to tell them, since they have met Jesus himself on the road), though he implies they do (compare Matthew 28.10 and 16). Luke keeps the women in clear view.

And they are not believed! We are on the brink of joy, and instead find ourselves surrounded by male stupidity and prejudice! The reactions of the celebrated 'apostles' could not be more different from those of the women. The women have bowed themselves to the ground and worshipped. They have been in the presence of the holy, and have recognized it at once. They have remembered Jesus' words, and for the first time understood them; at last they have sunk in. And they have come straight back from the tomb to tell everyone – as if they could do anything else! And then the apostles dismiss their story as complete nonsense.

Why? The second-century theologian Origen reports the reaction of an educated pagan called Celsus to the story of the resurrection (it does not matter that he seems chiefly to have John's version in mind): 'after death he rose again and showed the marks of his punishment and how his hands had been pierced. But who saw this? A hysterical female, as you say, and perhaps some other one of those who were deluded by the same sorcery' (Origen, *Contra Celsum*, 2.55). Is that it? Do the apostles regard these women they know so well, and with whom they have been through so much, as hysterical females? Are they taking it out on them, because they feel ashamed they did not share their courage when it came to the crucifixion; the women did not desert Jesus, but they did? That last speculation smacks too much, perhaps, of modern psychology, though we are still free to imagine that is what is going on in the apostles' heads. Closer to Luke's and the apostles' world was the idea that God or his angels did not communicate reliably with women. This is the explanation Bauckham prefers (*Gospel Women*, pp. 269–76). The Bible almost everywhere shares or inculcates that view. God has a very great deal to say to Abraham; all he says to Abraham's wife Sarah is 'Yes, you did laugh', just three words in the Hebrew of Genesis 18.15. He lets Moses into the secrets of his mind, and gives him whole books of them to hand on to the people of Israel; though Moses' sister Miriam is given high status in the narrative, God has but three verses for her, and that in the form of a sharp and devastating rebuke (Numbers 12.6–8, and see the result in verse 10, where Miriam suddenly becomes leprous). We have many books full of the words of male prophets; only in one short passage in 2 Kings 22.14–20 (reproduced with slightly different wording in 2 Chronicles 34.22–38) do we hear a pronouncement from a prophetess. There are glorious exceptions to this rule: the stories of Hagar in Genesis 16 and 21, for example, the first person in the Bible to 'see' God, and the only one anywhere to give him a new name; or the story of the unnamed wife of Manoah in Judges 13, who meets with God three times, and discovers he would far rather communicate with her than with her obtuse husband. Yet such passages are pitifully rare.

Until we reach the beginning of Luke's Gospel, that is. Coming to the Lukan birth stories from those in Matthew, we notice almost at once that Luke puts women centre stage. Mary is so far back in the shadows of Matthew's stories that we do not know whether like Joseph and the magi she understands the significance of her own son's birth. An angel appears three times in a dream to Joseph, always to impart sufficient wisdom or advice to turn the course of events (Matthew 1.20; 2.13, 19). He never has anything to say to Mary. At first in Luke's birth narratives, when the angel Gabriel appears to the priest Zechariah in the temple (1.11–20), we might think his plot is running true to the old form. But then Gabriel appears a second time, to announce the birth of Jesus himself, and this time it is to Mary. She and her cousin Elizabeth become the dominant characters for a crucial part of the narrative (1.26–61), and it is Joseph who is and who remains in the shadows. When the shepherds run to see her son and find the truth of what the angels have told them, they find not 'Joseph and Mary', as convention would lead us to expect, but 'Mary and Joseph' (2.16). Mary comes first in Luke.

So if 'the apostles' in his story think that heaven only communicates with men, Luke does not agree with them. He does not immediately pass judgement on them. He will leave that to the risen Jesus in his story of the journey to Emmaus (see 24.24–25).

At least Peter goes to the tomb. It seems he is not so dismissive as the rest. He does not take the women's report on trust, nor does he share their insight and belief. But they have made him wonder. He must go and see for himself. The story of Emmaus that follows this one will tell us he does not go alone (see 24.24). For now Luke's attention is focussed entirely on him, so that his companions are entirely invisible.

The episode is afforded but one verse. Luke has very little to report. When Peter reaches the tomb, the angels are gone. He peers inside the tomb, and finds not the divine, but the signs of burial. That is all. He goes away perplexed, and the Emmaus story will make clear his companions share his bewilderment. The women remain isolated in their experience of the divine, and in their understanding of Jesus' teaching about his death and resurrection. Perhaps Peter and his companions are on their way towards belief (and a few others, also; the Emmaus story will suggest that is the case), but for the moment the little community is divided, and the women are left in a corner, effectively silenced, regarded by most of their friends as purveyors of nonsense.

John – Mary of Magdala, and . . . ?

Before we travel to Emmaus ourselves, we must explore the last and indubitably the greatest of all the stories of the women at the tomb, the story of Mary of Magdala in John.

> Early on the first day, while it was still dark, Mary Magdalene came to the tomb. She saw that the stone had been moved away from the tomb. So she went running to Simon Peter and the other disciple, the one whom Jesus loved, and said to them, 'They have taken the Lord out of the tomb, and we do not know where they have put him!' (20.1–2)

That is how the story begins. John has mentioned Mary of Magdala at the cross (19.25), but not at the burial. And yet now, as we have already observed, Mary seems to know exactly where the tomb is and can find her way there even in the dark. John's description does not make sense unless we presume she has accompanied Joseph and Nicodemus in their sorry procession, and perhaps has played her part in the preparation of Jesus' corpse.

Is she now on her own? It would seem so until she reports back to Simon Peter and the beloved disciple, and says, 'We do not know where they have laid him.' It seems John knows the tradition of two or more women coming to the tomb, and is reflecting it here. But he is also following his usual habit of focussing the narrative down on the main characters. In this beginning to the passage he is clearing the way for Mary's second visit to the tomb, where she will be entirely on her own, and where the dramatic intensity of her encounter with the risen Jesus is much enhanced as a result.

Yet this means we have another woman or other women deep in the shadows of John's narrative. We cannot give them any names, unless we borrow them from the other Gospels. Do they too run back with Mary to Simon Peter and the other disciple? John does not even tell us that. Presumably they do, but what do they do next? We do not know, for they leave the stage, making it free, in a few verses' time, for Mary and her big scene. They are only present in that one phrase, 'we do not know', just two words in John's Greek.

And yet we must not think this is the last we hear of them. In the passage following the one where Mary encounters Jesus, he appears to 'the disciples' (20.19). That does not just mean the Twelve; its reference is wider than that. John's writing invites us to imagine this unnamed woman or women being there with the others.

The other three Gospels give their own prominence to Mary of Magdala. In their lists of the women at the crucifixion, burial and empty tomb they always put her name at the head of the list. She must have played a leading role, indeed *the* leading role in both the formation and dissemination of the tradition of the crucifixion, burial and resurrection, and must surely have been a major figure in the very early Church. Yet we would not now begin to give her the attention we do, if it were not for John. It is his account that makes her stand out from the crowd, and puts such colour in her cheeks.

At first, however, he seems to diminish her role. He does not explain in so many words, for starters, why she goes to the tomb. Matthew does not make the women's motives clear, either, but he leaves the possibility open, as we have seen, that they go to anoint the body and so complete the burial. But John closes that option. Alone of all the Gospel writers he tells us that Joseph of Arimathea is assisted in the burial by Nicodemus and that Nicodemus brings with him 'a mixture of myrrh and aloes, weighing about a hundred pounds' (19.39). One hundred pounds of extremely costly spices, even if we call it 75 pounds (the Roman pound was three quarters the size of ours), is a vast amount. As commentators have remarked, it is fit for a king. John also tells us the burial is done 'in accordance with Jewish burial custom' (19.40). So everything is done properly, with no expense spared, and on a scale astonishingly lavish for a peasant teacher and healer from Nazareth, let alone one who has just died a criminal's death.

So why do Mary and her companion(s) return to the tomb, and with such urgency, not even waiting for the sun to light their way? The only reason left to us is their grief and the need to express it as close as possible to the person they have lost. That is confirmed for us by the beginning of the scene in which Mary and Jesus meet: 'But Mary stood outside the tomb weeping' (20.11). It is the only explicit reference to grieving that we find in any of the resurrection stories.

So Mary and her companion(s) come to the tomb because they cannot bear to let Jesus go. They do not expect to be able to do anything but weep, and they will not even be able to let their tears fall on Jesus' body, because the tomb has been sealed. But still they come, and earlier than the women in any of the other Gospels.

When they get there, the opportunity for them to be close to Jesus once again is denied them, for the stone has been removed, and the body is gone. The pace of John's narrative is so fast here that he does not speak of the women entering the tomb, or even just looking into it. But look in they must, for they discover the body has gone, and having looked in, surely they will have entered to make quite sure. They find no angel, as the women do in the other Gospels. When she comes to the tomb again, then Mary will find angels, but for now there is nothing, and loss is piled on loss. What do they think? Not that the grave has been robbed, for why should she say to Simon and the beloved disciple, 'We do not know where they have laid him', and why later should she say the same to the figure she takes for the gardener (20.13)? It appears she thinks someone must have decided that Jesus is buried in 'the wrong place', and therefore has removed his body to somewhere 'more suitable'. That he has been buried at all might surprise some, for the bodies of crucified men were sometimes left unburied for the wild animals and birds to eat, just so the humiliation of the death could be made complete. That he is buried in a rich man's tomb – Joseph's tomb is of a kind very few people could afford – close, no doubt to the tombs of other wealthy and powerful families, would strike many as shocking and quite unacceptable. So Mary seems to fear that Jesus has been summarily buried somewhere else, among the poor or, worse, has been left with the rubbish to rot.

No wonder she and her companion(s) run away and wake up Simon and the beloved disciple. They have not yet begun to find the meaning of it all. They have not yet stumbled upon the divine. No angels have appeared. They are frightened and bewildered, drowning in bitter grief.

The two male disciples run to the tomb to see for themselves:

> Peter and the other disciple went out and started to go to the tomb. The two of them were running together, but the other disciple was faster and outran Peter, and reached the tomb first. Peering inside, he saw the linen wrappings lying there, but he did not go in. Then Simon Peter came along behind him and went straight into the tomb. He saw the wrappings lying there, and the piece of cloth that had covered his head, not lying with the wrappings, but rolled up in a place by itself. Then the other disciple, the one who had reached the tomb first, also went inside, and he saw, and believed. (They did not yet understand the scripture, that Jesus had to rise from the dead.) Then the disciples went back home.
>
> (20.3–10)

Almost all of this is incidental detail, introduced by John to set things up for the crucial scene where Jesus will appear. The beloved disciple's outrunning Peter does not turn the going to the tomb into a race. They are simply running as hard as they can, because Mary's report is so disturbing, and 'the other disciple' happens to be the faster of the two. But it means that John can heighten the drama of their arrival at the tomb. The other disciple arrives first, but does not go inside; he simply peers in and sees the wrappings. Peter goes straight in, and finds not just the wrappings, but the head cloth rolled up by itself. (Some comment on Peter's impetuosity, but his entering the tomb is hardly surprising. What might seem strange is the other disciple's *not* immediately going in, but that too is surely for dramatic effect.) Once Peter is inside, he follows, and then, 'He saw and believed'.

This is the only point in the passage where John moves from what is incidental towards what is central. To Peter the tomb makes no sense. It means little more to the other disciple at first. Peering in, he sees but an empty tomb. Once inside, however, does he come to know what it must be like for the high priest on the Day of Atonement to go behind the curtain of the sanctuary of the temple, and enter the Holy of Holies?

Soon Mary of Magdala will find two angels sitting on the burial shelf, one where the head of Jesus has been, the other at the feet. Once upon a time, before it was captured and taken to Babylon, the ark of the covenant had lain in the Holy of Holies in the temple, and over that had been the mercy seat, flanked by two winged cherubim (see Exodus 25.10–22). Above that God was enthroned. 'You who are enthroned upon the cherubim, shine forth', writes the poet in Psalm 80.1b; 'He sits enthroned upon the cherubim; let the earth quake!' cries the composer of Psalm 99.1b. Yet the God of Israel was not represented by a statue of any kind. He was invisibly enthroned. There was nothing to see, but the human trappings of his presence and, in Herod's temple, the one still being finished when Jesus died, there was nothing at all, no statue, no furniture. The ark, the mercy seat, the cherubim had never been recovered. The Holy of Holies was empty. But of course, it was not, not in the belief of the high priest, or the priests, or all devout Jews. It was full of God.

And is that how 'the other disciple' finds the tomb, when he goes inside: full of God? Is that what his seeing and believing mean? The movement of John's drama, written with conscious literary skill, suggests they might well *begin* to mean that, but only begin. The beloved disciple, for all his own love for Jesus, does not meet him in the tomb. He does not meet with God. To use again that wonderful line from R. S. Thomas' poem 'Alive', he can but say, 'I find the place where you lay warm.' He does not meet the divine, because Mary will be the one to do that, just four verses later. Her encounter will provide the climax to the whole piece, and the experience of the beloved disciple inside the tomb but prepares the way for it. The meeting is still a great surprise when it comes, to Mary, and to us, too, the readers of this Gospel.

> But Mary stood outside the tomb weeping. As she wept, she peered into the tomb, and saw two angels in white sitting there, one at the head, the other at the feet, where the body of Jesus had lain. They said to her, 'Woman, why are you weeping?' She said to them, 'They have taken away my Lord, and I do not know where they have laid him.' Having said this, she turned round and saw Jesus standing there. But she did not realize it was Jesus. Jesus said to her, 'Woman, why are you weeping? Who are you looking for?' Supposing he was the gardener, she said to him, 'Sir, if you are the one who has carried him away, tell me where you have laid him, and I will go and take him away.' Jesus said to her, 'Mary!' She turned and said to him in Hebrew, 'Rabbouni!' (which means Teacher). Jesus said to her, 'Do not touch me, for I have not yet ascended to the Father. But go to my brothers and sisters and tell them, "I am ascending to my Father and your Father, to my God and your God."' Mary of Magdala went and announced to the disciples, 'I have seen the Lord!' She told them what he had said to her.
>
> (John 20.11–18)

So Mary has run back to the tomb, also. In the previous passage we might have imagined just two figures running, but there were three. True to his usual form, John has focussed on the characters of the moment and neglected anyone else. It is all for dramatic effect, and again it works. At what point does Mary arrive on the scene? When the two men are inside the tomb? After they have turned for home? We are free to imagine what we like, so long as we give due weight to her grief. If the beloved disciple has shared with anyone the insight he has gained, it has not been with Mary, or at least she has not been able to grasp it. John's story is most easily understood, of course, if we think of that disciple keeping what he has found to himself for the time being.

The two men's leaving is not reprehensible. It is not remotely like their deserting Jesus in his hour of need. In any case, in John's story of the crucifixion, the beloved disciple does not desert him, but is there to the end with the women. Yet now they do not stay. Peter goes away bewildered; the beloved disciple knows the truth, but does not wait to meet with it. He leaves the stage free for Mary. That is remarkable. John has not told us a great deal about this second disciple but, by the description he uses of him, 'the one whom Jesus loved', and by speaking of him reclining next to Jesus at the meal when Jesus washes his disciples' feet and tells them of his coming betrayal and arrest (13.23), John builds a picture of a very particular bond between them. That bond is strengthened just before Jesus dies. Looking from the cross and seeing his mother and the disciple standing there, Jesus says to his mother, 'Woman, here is your son,' and to the disciple, 'Here is your mother.' John comments, 'And from that hour the disciple took her into his own home' (19.26–27). By the conventions of the day, in taking Mary to his home, the disciple establishes a new household. This is the moment when the new family of the Church is formally begun, with Mary signifying the ideal female disciple, and the beloved disciple representing the ideal male disciple. Mary of Magdala is not singled out at that point. In all the lists of the women at the crucifixion, burial or empty tomb in the other Gospels, her name always appears first. But not in John's list of those at the cross: 'Standing near the cross of Jesus were his mother and his mother's sister, Mary the wife of Clopas, and Mary of Magdala' (19.25). True, the beloved disciple is not even mentioned there, but it is the very next verse which talks of Jesus seeing him and his mother and which brings him to such prominence. Mary of Magdala, who has never appeared in John's Gospel before, and who is not described, as she is in the other Gospels, as having accompanied Jesus from Galilee, is last in the list of women, and is given no individual role to play.

So it is against all expectations that she should be the one who stays behind when Peter and the beloved disciple leave, and that she should be the person to whom Jesus appears. She

steps out of the deep shadows of the narrative, where for so
long she has been completely invisible, to take centre stage.
Suddenly it appears that she, not Simon Peter, nor Mary of
Nazareth, nor even the beloved disciple, is the one who is most
devoted to Jesus. Her grief, by the terms of John's story, runs
deeper than theirs. It binds her to the tomb, though there is
nothing for her to do there but weep.

Her devotion is richly rewarded. *Now* the angels appear.
Suddenly the tomb is no longer empty. It is not just the place
where he lay warm. It is full of heaven. Yet Mary's eyes are
too full of tears, it seems, to recognize it. When the angels ask
why she is crying, she remains consumed by her sense of loss.
She does not bend her face to the ground, as she and the other
women do in Luke. She is not overcome with fear and awe,
as they are in Luke's account, and in Mark's and Matthew's.
She continues to speak as she did when she ran back to Simon
Peter and the beloved disciple. All she wants to know is 'where
they have laid him'.

And still that remains the case after she turns round, sees
Jesus standing near her, and hears him repeat the question,
'Why are you weeping?' She does not recognize him. She does
not recognize his voice. She thinks he must be the gardener.
She misses the divine altogether. It seems quite extraordinary,
as if John is straining too hard here for dramatic effect. Yet,
of course, missing the divine when it is staring us in the face,
or not recognizing God's voice, is a commonplace of human
experience. We do it all the time, even if our faith runs deep.
Mary is not the 'hysterical female' of Celsus' misogynist comment. She is simply human. And of course, as John has been
keen to emphasize, she is sunk in grief. She is simply unable
to see or think straight.

Until, that is, Jesus calls her name.

In his famous exposition of 'the good shepherd' John has
Jesus say this: 'The one who enters by the gate is shepherd of
the sheep. For him the gatekeeper opens the gate, and the
sheep hear his voice, and he calls his own sheep by name and
leads them out . . . the sheep follow him. Because they know
his voice' (10.2–3, 4b). We have to imagine a Palestinian shepherd coming to the village pens, where the flocks of several

families are held for the night, to lead his own animals out to pasture and water. He does not need to lay his hands on his own family's animals to separate them from the rest. He only needs to call out their names.

So it now becomes clear that Mary of Magdala belongs to Jesus' 'flock'. She must have been with him for some considerable time, as the other Gospels say. After all, she cannot really have popped up out of nowhere to stand near Jesus at the cross, even if John's narrative, shaped and constrained by the demands of dramatic storytelling, has had her doing just that.

The calling of her name shakes her out of grief into joy, but of itself it does not bring her to full recognition of Jesus. She knows now he is not the gardener, but she thinks he is simply her 'teacher', her 'rabbi'. Overjoyed, and without wondering how he could possibly have come back to life, she reaches out to touch him. But Jesus is not her old friend come back to life. He belongs to the world of the divine and, even as he speaks, he is putting on the clothes of divinity. He is, as John puts it, 'ascending to the Father'. He is, we might say, betwixt and between, if such talk makes any sense at all.

For John the 'ascension' is not a separate event, as Luke seems to make it in the first chapter of Acts, and as the Church celebrates it in its liturgical year. For John the crucifixion, resurrection and ascension are all one. Together they represent Jesus' 'hour', the moment when he 'goes to the Father', when his glory is revealed, when the veil is torn aside and he emerges as God. There is no separate transfiguration story in John, as there is in each of the other three Gospels. He does not need one. The story of Jesus' death, resurrection and ascension is enough; *there* lies Jesus' transfiguration. 'When you lift up the Son of Man,' Jesus says in 8.28, 'then you will know that I am.' Again we hear that mysterious 'I am', the divine name, taken from the 'I am the One who is' of Exodus 3.14. As Raymond Brown says in the first volume of his great commentary on John, Jesus' ascent in John is in three stages: first he is 'lifted up from the earth' on the cross (see 12.32–33), then he is raised up from death, and finally he is lifted up to heaven (Anchor Bible, *The Gospel According to John*, vol. 1, I–XII, 1966, p. 146).

Mary has not quite caught up with events. She finds Jesus, or rather he finds her, at the point where the process of his being 'lifted up' is nearly complete. The final stage is upon him. Yet she still calls him 'rabbi', and wishes to hold on to him. She must let him go. To have him as her God, she must set her old friend free. To call him Lord, she must bid her rabbi farewell. This is why Jesus tells her not to touch him. With Thomas, in the next scene but one, it will be different. There Jesus will invite him to 'touch' him, precisely so that he may find the intimacy that will convince him that this wounded Jesus is indeed his Lord and his God.

Thomas does not need to 'touch' Jesus. The invitation to do so is sufficient. Jesus' words to Mary are also enough to bring her to the heart of the truth. By not touching, both Thomas and Mary suddenly find their God within touching distance. When Mary rushes back to the other disciples, she says not, 'I have seen our rabbi!' but, 'I have seen the Lord!'

Her own ascent into truth has happened in stages. John does not tell us her reactions to the crucifixion, but she is sufficiently moved by it to accompany Joseph and Nicodemus to the burial, and then to be drawn and drawn again to the tomb. Then comes the second stage at the tomb, not with the appearance of the angels, but with Jesus' calling her name. She finds him again, but still does not see him for who he is. The third stage comes as Jesus speaks of his ascension and sends her to his brothers and sisters. Now she has found her God, her Lord; she has *seen* him, and he has called her by name. We do not need to know anything else. Nor does she.

'Am I not an apostle?' Paul asks the Christians of Corinth. 'Have I not seen Jesus our Lord?' (1 Corinthians 9.1). In Paul's view what made him an apostle, or one who had been sent (that is what the word literally means), was his encounter with the risen Christ, his 'seeing the Lord', and his being commissioned by him to share that encounter and all it meant with others. On these grounds Mary of Magdala is often called 'the apostle to the apostles' by those who seek to do her honour. Yet, as Bauckham has pointed out (*Gospel Women*, p. 285), that title is not good enough. For it suggests that once she has reported everything to the other disciples, her work is done, and she can leave it to them, especially the Eleven, especially the men, to carry things further. We will come to John's story of Jesus' appearance to 'the disciples' in the chapter after next, but we have already suggested we should imagine Mary as being among them. If we do, then she will be commissioned with the others. We have also speculated about the leading role she must have played in the early Church. Only on that basis can we understand the part she plays in all four Gospels in the stories of Jesus' death and resurrection. John's story of her beside the tomb in particular surely cannot be explained any other way.

So, if we are to use Pauline criteria for the definition of an apostle, then Mary of Magdala is not so much the apostle to the apostles as the first apostle. Men in positions of power in the contemporary Church, particularly those who accord so much importance to the apostolic succession, might pay heed to that!

3

Two meals and a piece of broiled fish

―▶◆◀―

Entertaining God; being entertained by God

Among the resurrection stories we find two concerning meals. The first one we shall explore is Luke's famous story of the journey to Emmaus. The second, in John, is set beside the Sea of Galilee, and contains what is, by my reckoning, one of the great lines of Scripture. In between, we shall turn briefly to Luke's little story of the piece of broiled fish – not his finest hour!

But first we must set the two stories of the meals against the background of the Hebrew Bible, and its own talk of entertaining God or being entertained by him.

One of its most extraordinary passages we have quoted already, in the course of our discussion of the transfiguration story. It is less than three verses long and is worth quoting again:

> Moses went up, and with him Aaron, Nadab, and Abihu and seventy of the elders of Israel. And they saw the God of Israel, and beneath his feet was like a fashioning of sapphire pavement and like the very heavens for pureness . . . and they beheld God and ate and drank.
>
> (Exodus 24.9–11, Alter's translation)

If such writing is peculiarly bold – and it is; there is very little like it in the whole Bible – then Genesis 18 is even more adventurous, for it speaks of entertaining God. Admittedly, Abraham and Sarah do not understand what they are doing, for they do not recognize the three strangers who turn up at

their tents in the heat of the day, but think they are simply
human travellers in need of shade, refreshment for their tired
feet, and food and drink:

> And the Lord appeared to him [that is Abraham] in the
> Terebinths of Mamre when he was sitting by the tent flap
> in the heat of the day. And he raised his eyes and saw,
> and look, three men were standing before him. He saw,
> and ran toward them from the tent flap and bowed to
> the ground. And he said, 'My lord, if I have found favour
> in your eyes, please do not go on past your servant. Let
> a little water be fetched and bathe your feet and stretch
> out under the tree, and let me fetch a morsel of bread,
> and refresh yourselves. Then you may go on, for have
> you not come by your servant?' And they said, 'Do as
> you have spoken.' And Abraham hurried to the tent to
> Sarah and he said, 'Hurry! Knead three *seahs* of choice
> semolina flour and make loaves.' And to the herd
> Abraham ran and fetched a tender and goodly calf and
> gave it to the lad, who hurried to prepare it. And he
> fetched curds and milk and the calf that had been pre-
> pared and he set these before them, he standing over
> them under the tree, and they ate.
>
> (Genesis 18.1–8, Alter's translation)

The opening words of this passage, 'The Lord appeared to
him', make clear who it is who has come in need of Abraham's
hospitality, at least the identity of one of the figures. It is none
other than God himself. The other two figures, as the narrative will eventually make clear, are heavenly companions
of his. We might suppose it becomes a recognition scene, and
that in the following verses Abraham, Sarah and the lad will
realize who the guests are. But this is Genesis, and its colourful storytelling is capable of mixing the profound with rich
humour. This is one of the most sublime passages of all; it
is also one of the funniest. The hosts never do penetrate the
disguise, and whether or not the young servant lad does,
we are not told for, alas, he is only a young servant lad and
does not seem to count for anything.

There is one more passage we should quote before we return to the Gospels, and this time it is poetry, from what is one of the most famous and best-loved poems in all Scripture, Psalm 23. It is chiefly known for its image of God the shepherd, and the way that is developed. Those opening four verses deserve all the praise given to them, but in my mind they are followed by two verses that are even more remarkable:

> You spread a table before me
> in front of my enemies.
> You anoint my head with oil;
> my cup runs over.
>
> Surely goodness and faithful love pursue me
> all the days of my life
> and I shall dwell in the house of the Eternal forever.
> (Psalm 23. 5–6, Jonathan Magonet's translation, from
> *A Rabbi Reads the Psalms*, 2nd edn, 2004, p. 48)

God is no longer the shepherd, guarding his sheep as they walk through the valley of the shadow of death. He is host, the provider of a lavish, joyful banquet, a bright token of his 'goodness and faithful love'. He waits upon his guests, pouring sweet-scented oil over their heads and faces, treating them as if they were royalty and this was their coronation, and filling their glasses so full with wine that it overflows. And those who sing or pray this song tell of God doing all this in front of their enemies. The earlier verses of the psalm have spoken of the dangers they have endured, the possible dangers they still face. For the people of the time, especially their men, one of the greatest risks they ran was losing their honour. The song's penultimate verse gains meaning and power, if we imagine the 'enemies' having put those who pray its lines to great shame. They have found themselves in the gutter (a less poetic version of 'the valley of the shadow of death' of verse 4). But now look at them! Sitting down at God's table, treated like kings and queens, with God waiting on them, the perfumes of heaven glistening on their heads, and God's finest vintage brimming over their cups! Could any higher honour be accorded to them? No wonder they speak of dwelling in the house of God forever!

With these lines still echoing in our ears, and those two stories from Exodus and Genesis, too, let us set out for Emmaus.

Emmaus

The scene is set by Luke's story of the women at the tomb, of their meeting with the angels and their finding the truth of Jesus' resurrection, and then having their report dismissed by the apostles as nonsense. There has been no meeting with the risen Jesus himself. Though with the angels the women have found themselves in the presence of the divine, they have not met Jesus on the way back to the other disciples, nor have they lingered by the tomb and encountered him there. Matthew's story of the meeting on the road has not been told, nor any story to compare with John's of Mary of Magdala. Peter and his companions have gone to the tomb, but have found nothing but some burial cloths. The narrative is crying out for some resolution.

> Now see, two of them on that same day were walking to a village called Emmaus, about seven miles from Jerusalem. They were talking with each other about all these things that had happened. Now it happened, while they were talking and discussing, Jesus drew near and began to walk with them. But their eyes were kept from recognizing him. He said to them, 'What is all this you are exchanging with one another as you walk along?' They stopped, their faces sad. One of them, whose name was Cleopas, answered and said to him, 'Are you the only stranger in Jerusalem who does not know what happened there these last few days?' 'What things?' he said. They replied, 'The things concerning Jesus of Nazareth. He was a prophet, powerful in deed and word before God and all the people. Our chief priests and leaders handed him over to be condemned to death and they crucified him.

As for us, we were hoping that he was the one who would deliver Israel. Besides all this, it is now the third day since all this happened. There's more. Some women from our company astounded us. They went to the tomb early this morning and failed to find his body. They came back saying they had had a vision of angels, who told them he was alive. Then some of our number went off to the tomb, and found it exactly as the women had said, but they did not see him.' Then he said to them, 'How obdurate you are, how slow of heart to believe all the prophets have said! Was it not necessary for the Messiah to suffer these things and then enter into his glory?' Then, beginning with Moses and all the prophets, he interpreted for them the things written about him in every part of the Scriptures.

They had drawn near the village they were walking to, and he made as if he was going to carry on walking. But they urged him strongly, saying, 'Stay with us, for it is nearly evening, and the day is already far spent.' So he went in to stay with them. Now it happened that when he was at the table with them, he took the bread, pronounced a blessing, broke it, and gave it to them. Then their eyes were opened and they recognized him. Then he vanished from their sight. They said to one another, 'Were not our hearts on fire as he spoke with us on the road, when he opened the Scriptures to us?' Getting up that same hour they returned to Jerusalem. They found the Eleven and the others gathered together. They were saying, 'It is true! The Lord has risen and has appeared to Simon!' Then they recounted what had taken place on the road, and how he was revealed to them in the breaking of the bread. (Luke 24.13–35)

The angel at the tomb in Mark tells the women to go with the other disciples to Galilee: 'There you will see him', he says. The angel in Matthew says the same, and the appearance of Jesus so soon after leaving the tomb comes as a complete surprise. But in John 20 Mary of Magdala has met Jesus beside his tomb, and in the second half of that chapter he meets his other disciples in Jerusalem, on the evening of the day of resurrection, and they are still in Jerusalem a week later when he appears to Thomas. Only then do we move to Galilee, where Jesus appears beside the Sea of Tiberias.

Luke never does go to Galilee. He remains in and around Jerusalem, and even when soon he tells of Jesus' ascension, he takes us only a very short distance from the city, as far as the village of Bethany. His Gospel begins in Jerusalem, in the very sanctuary of its temple, with Zechariah the good priest; Jesus is born in Bethlehem, only some five miles from the city, and the last we hear of him before he enters upon the public stage, he is back in the temple as a 12-year-old boy, astounding the teachers there with his wisdom. The first chapters of his adult ministry are set in Galilee, but then we hear in 9.51, soon after the story of the transfiguration, that 'he set his face to go to Jerusalem'. After that the narrative brings us inexorably closer and closer to the city, until in Luke 19 Jesus enters it in triumph. But then he causes mayhem in the temple precincts, protests that the temple reduces those who have next to nothing to abject poverty, and foretells its destruction, and Jerusalem's, also. He is arrested by the Jewish authorities, mocked, beaten, sent on to Pilate, the Roman procurator, then to Herod, and finally sentenced by Pilate to death by crucifixion.

These are the things that Cleopas and his companion tell the stranger who meets them on the road.

Of the four Gospel writers, Luke and John are the most sophisticated in the art of storytelling. In this story of Emmaus it is clear that Luke is striving hard for dramatic effect. And he most certainly succeeds! He has produced a masterpiece, and one that stands alongside John's story of Mary of Magdala at the tomb in the affections of Christians.

Its pace seems relaxed: 13 of its 23 verses are devoted to direct speech, all but three of those to dialogue. Yet Luke has here distilled much of the deepest experience of the earliest of Jesus' followers.

The impact of the passage depends a great deal on the suspense Luke creates and the irony he employs. Suspense is created at the very beginning. When in Acts 2 Luke arrives at his story of the festival of Pentecost in Jerusalem and the filling of the disciples with the Holy Spirit, he starts with this: 'When the day of Pentecost had come, they were all together in one place' (Acts 2.1). Here, however, we find two disciples already leaving Jerusalem for their home in Emmaus. It is still only the afternoon of the day of resurrection or, as Cleopas puts it, 'the third day since all this happened'. Is the community already beginning to break up and disperse? It would seem so.

What the intentions of Cleopas and his companion are for the longer term, we are not told. They talk about members of 'our company', and retain a strong sense of belonging. Yet that 'company' is already seriously split. There are the women, Mary of Magdala, Joanna, Mary the mother of James, and the rest, who have found the tomb empty, who have met with angels, who understand what Jesus was teaching them before he died, who have tumbled to the truth. But they have been dismissed as fools. Some, perhaps the majority, do not trust the women's story, seem to be stuck in their shattering sense of loss, and appear to be fast *un*learning what Jesus has taught them. There is enough in all the Gospels, and in Luke in particular, to suggest that Jesus himself ascribed equal honour to both men and women (and indeed children), and gave them a dignity and a status they had never had before: like the men, the women and children counted as children of God, precious members of God's household; they were able to call him 'Father' and to appeal to him direct without going through the priests or other members of the religious establishment; they were surrounded at all times and on all occasions by God's forgiveness and mercy, and by his strong, utterly dependable love. Some members of 'the company' seem to have reverted back to type and, in the shock of Jesus' death, are busy re-erecting the barriers he went to such lengths to overturn.

In between that group and the women are Peter and other disciples who have accompanied him (we now learn from this Emmaus story) to the tomb. They are not yet where the women are. Their eyes are not so far open. They have had no vision of angels, yet they have stepped on to the road that will take them to the truth. They have learned that the women were not speaking nonsense, although they have not yet seen what they saw. For the time being they are simply bewildered. To what group do Cleopas and his companion belong at the point where they set out for Emmaus? We cannot be quite sure. They have not been to the tomb with Peter, and yet they seem to agree he has begun to make the women's story believable, and to share his bewilderment. They have not fled back to the trenches of their old ideas and attitudes, and yet they are leaving for home, as if it is all over, as if the crucifixion has marked the end of the dream and of the great task they have been involved in of building the kingdom of God. The kingdoms of Pilate and the high priest have triumphed after all. Is that what they think? And yet their heads are buzzing with the stories of the women and of Peter and his companions. They are 'talking and discussing' on the road, not walking along in sullen silence. Perhaps it is not all over. Perhaps . . .

Who is Cleopas' companion? Are we to think of a man or a woman? At the climax of the story the two invite Jesus to stay the night with them, so presumably they are members of the same household. It could be Cleopas' brother or sister, but perhaps the most natural thing is to think of them as husband and wife. Nothing in Luke's description of them gets in the way of that idea. It was just that he only knew the name of one of them. Cleopas is a shortened version of Cleopatrus, which itself is the masculine version of Cleopatra. While it is sorely tempting to call the two of them Cleopas and Cleopatra, we had better rest content with 'Cleopas and his wife', and that is how we will refer to them from now on, knowing full well that Luke himself is not so definite.

And now the risen Jesus meets them on their small journey. When the slave Hagar runs away from Sarah's cruelty, God meets her beside a spring of water in the desert called Beer-lahai-roi (Genesis 16.7–14). When Jacob flees to Haran from his brother Esau's murderous threats, God meets him on the way at Bethel (Genesis 28.10–22), and again, 20 years later, at the wadi Jabbok as he returns (Genesis 32.22–32). In all three cases recognition comes at the end of the encounter. Hagar cries, 'You are El-roi!' (16.13), as if she has suddenly realized that the strange figure she can see and hear is none other than God. Quite what her 'roi' means, we do not know for certain, probably 'the one who sees me'. But 'El' is clear as clear: it is the common Hebrew word for God. So Hagar's Hebrew might plausibly be translated, 'You are God-Who-Sees-Me!' At Bethel God appears to Jacob while he is asleep. When he wakes up, then he exclaims: 'Heavens above! The Lord is in this place, and I did not know!' (28.16). Though at the Jabbok he wrestles with God all night, it is not until the brink of dawn when the struggle is over that he comes to his senses: 'Jacob called the name of the place Peniel, Face-of-God', the story goes, ' "For," he said, "I have seen God face to face, and my life has been saved!" ' (32.30). Poetic stories such as these, so powerful and so deep-rooted in the Jewish memory and soul, so deep-rooted in Luke, established or helped maintain a certain etiquette: when writing of an encounter with God, better have it not sink in straightaway; let there be sudden recognition at the end. Not only will that make for more effective drama, it will do greater justice to the overwhelming mystery of God. The women in Matthew recognize the risen Jesus at once. John and Luke, master storytellers that they are, do it differently: Mary of Magdala at first takes Jesus for the gardener; Cleopas and his wife do not recognize him till he is inside their home, at their meal table, and until he does something which is so unusual, yet so familiar.

Yet looking back from that new vantage point, they can see it beginning to dawn on them back on the road: ' "Were not our hearts on fire," they say to one another, "as he spoke with us on the road, when he opened the Scriptures to us?" ' Now they can identify two things that have revealed the risen Jesus to them, his reinterpreting the Scriptures, as well as his breaking of the bread.

The Gospels themselves, and indeed the rest of the New Testament, bear eloquent testimony to the sophisticated re-interpretation of the Jewish Scriptures conducted by the earliest Christians, as they wrestled with the life, death and resurrection of Jesus of Nazareth. In our companion volume to this one, *The Christmas Stories* (2007), we began to explore the intricate web of passages from the Jewish Scriptures behind both Matthew's and Luke's series of stories on Jesus' birth. Those passages supplied the fabric on which Matthew and Luke embroidered their own wonderful tales. In this volume we have spoken of the stories and poems of the Jewish Scriptures beneath the surface of the Gospel stories of the transfiguration, the calming of the storm, the walking on the sea, and the feeding of the five thousand. When it came to the crucifixion, the need for reinterpretation was both especially urgent and difficult. Though the suffering of God is a major theme in the Jewish Scriptures, there was nothing that prepared anyone for a Messiah who would 'suffer these things', as the Emmaus story puts it. Yet, when they turned the light of the risen Christ on such passages concerning God's 'Servant' as Isaiah 50.4–9 or 52.13–53.12, or on the lament psalms, such as Psalms 22 or 69, it was as if they could see the words for the first time. Of course! How could they have been so blind, so stupid! Now everything fell into place! The Scriptures did not just point to Jesus, they even pointed to his crucifixion!

At first such realizations must have astonished both those who first entertained them, and those to whom they com-municated their discoveries. As time went on, the reinter-pretations became simply interpretations. The startlingly new became the norm. What Christians discovered became what Christians knew and believed. After a few decades the passages to which they returned time and time again, and the distinc-tively Christian telling of them, became deeply embedded in their thinking and storytelling and preaching. Read Isaiah 50.4–9 and 52.13–53.12 and Psalms 22 and 69 and then turn to the Gospels' accounts of the crucifixion of Jesus, and you will see what I mean.

By the time Luke wrote his story of the journey to Emmaus, those few decades had already passed. And yet, with remark-able skill, he manages to make fresh the memory of what it was like in those heady days of discovery, when the Scriptures suddenly burst into flame, and when they laughed at how blind and stupid they had been. 'Were not our hearts on fire as he spoke with us . . . when he opened the Scriptures to us?' Exactly!

But the moment of recognition does not come on the road. In that too Luke is accurately reflecting the experience of the early Christians. They did not reach the truth, the truth of the wounded God, by poring over their Scriptures till at last the penny dropped. The encounter with that God came first, and drove them back to the Scriptures. The encounter provided the motivation and the energy for their task of reinterpretation. In this story, despite Jesus having joined them on the way to their village, it is at the meal table, within the confines of their home, when they have stopped walking and have fallen silent, that they come to recognize who he is and the true meeting with him happens.

Thus far he has been twice a stranger to them: they have not known him as their friend and teacher, and they have also called him a 'stranger in Jerusalem'. To them he is an outsider, doubly so, for he belongs neither to their company, nor to the city near which they live and which has been the centre of their universe. 'Are you the only stranger in Jerusalem who does not know what happened there these last few days?' is a wonderful question to put to the one who has been at the centre of things! And then in a long speech they proceed to tell Jesus all the things he needs to know about himself! Cartloads of irony and a wry humour too! They also help to explain why this story still makes such an impact on those who hear it.

When Cleopas and his wife reach their village, the story changes character and becomes one of hospitality. Jesus makes as if he is going to carry on walking. Etiquette demands that he does not presume on their generosity. Genesis 19 tells of the visit of God's two companions from heaven to the city of Sodom. When they enter the city, they are met by Abraham's nephew Lot, as he is sitting in the gateway.

And Lot saw, and he rose to greet them and bowed, with his face to the ground. And he said, 'O please, my lords, turn aside to your servant's house to spend the night, and bathe your feet, and you can set off early on your way.' And they said, 'No. We will spend the night in the square.' And he pressed them hard, and they turned aside to him and came into his house, and he prepared them a feast and baked flatbread, and they ate.

(Genesis 19.1b–3, Alter's translation)

So Cleopas and his wife must offer shelter for the night and food and drink, while Jesus must at first politely refuse. Then they must press him, and he must accept. That way the proper courtesies are observed and everyone can relax.

The climax to the story comes when the meal is prepared and they are sitting down together to eat. At the beginning of this chapter we looked briefly at passages from the Jewish Scriptures concerning encounter with God that used the language of the meal. Meals are a vital part of the story of Jesus in all the Gospels, also, and Luke is no exception.

In 5.27–39 we learn of Jesus calling Levi, a collector of taxes for the Romans, to follow him, and how Levi then 'gave a great banquet in his house', where 'there was a large crowd of tax collectors and others sitting at the table with them'. The Pharisees and their scribes start muttering disapprovingly. 'Why do you eat and drink with tax collectors and sinners?' they ask the disciples. It is a good question. It gets to the heart of what Jesus is about. In their study, *Consuming Passions: The Anthropology of Eating* (1980, 4.211) Peter Farb and George Armelagos write:

In all societies, both simple and complex, eating is the primary way of initiating and maintaining human relationships . . . Once the anthropologist finds out where, when, and with whom the food is eaten, just about everything else can be inferred about the relations among the society's members . . . To know what, where, how, when, and with whom people eat is to know the character of their society.

We tend to start muttering disapprovingly ourselves about those Pharisees and their friends in Luke's story, but that is because we are not thinking hard enough, and because we do not recognize how truly shocking Jesus' practice was for his day. He put his stamp on his movement by the people he so gladly ate with, by his refusal to deny anyone a place in his circle and at his table, and by the new etiquette he taught. With a bright twinkle in the eye, he tells the people,

> When you are invited to a wedding banquet, do not go to recline on the top couch, in case someone more distinguished than you has been invited by your host; and the one who has invited both of you may come and say to you, 'Give this person your place,' and then in disgrace you have to get up to take the lowest place. Rather, when you are invited, go and lie at the lowest place, so that when your host comes, he might say to you, 'Friend, come up to a higher place.' (Luke 14.8–10a)

Behind the humour lies a radical vision. By poking fun at the ways in which people seek and maintain their honour and status, Jesus is in fact denying the validity of the search itself. The honour and status gained by being a child of God, a member of God's own family, is enough for anyone.

Just how far-reaching Jesus' vision was is made clearer in the very next passage in Luke: 'When you give a lunch or dinner, do not invite your friends or your brothers or your relatives or rich neighbours, in case they may invite you back, and you would then be repaid. But when you give a banquet, invite the poor, the crippled, the lame, the blind' (14.12b–13).

Both these passages are found only in Luke. The same is true of the story of Zacchaeus, the chief tax collector of Jericho, who climbs a tree to get a better view of Jesus as he is passing through the town. There is an astonishing moment when Jesus stops beneath the tree, looks up at Zacchaeus, and says to him, 'Zacchaeus, hurry and come down. I must stay at your house today' (19.5). As the chief tax collector, Zacchaeus will have lined his pockets at the grievous expense of the people. He will have driven some families into slavery, left others buried in debt. Luke tells us he is rich, and when he responds to Jesus' request, he makes clear he knows how much he has extorted from people and how much suffering he has caused (see 19.8). Luke's Jesus is not naïve. He will know exactly what kind of man Zacchaeus is, and how much he must be despised by the good people of Jericho. Jesus' own reputation has gone before him. Crowds of people have turned out to see him. He is a famous healer and teacher. For the sake of their own honour, and the honour of the town, the leading families of the town should offer him hospitality. But Jesus is one step ahead of them. Outrageously, he arranges his accommodation. It is outrageous because he invites himself; it is utterly outrageous because he invites himself to stay with a man like Zacchaeus, for in doing so he heaps great honour on the head of a man who hitherto has been both shameless and shamed.

We need to bear in mind these stories of Jesus' vision and practice as we bend our heads to enter the house in Emmaus, and wait as the meal is prepared. We need also to recall the stories of the feeding of the five thousand, and the Last Supper. In both of those Jesus takes bread, pronounces a blessing, breaks it and distributes it (see Luke 9.16 and 22.19).

Sometimes Luke has Jesus reclining at table to eat. That is the case at Levi's banquet, and again in the house of a Pharisee called Simon (the Greek of 5.29 or 7.36 and 7.37 makes it clear). But that was not Jesus' own style. As Crossan points out, reclining at table meant that one had to be served, and therefore was the practice of those who owned servants or slaves (*The Historical Jesus*, 1992, p. 403). Not only did Jesus have no slaves, he took it upon himself to do their work, as the story of his washing his disciples' feet in John 13.1–17 so eloquently reveals. He did not leave the serving of food to others. He did it himself. Crossan's further comment on the language of 'taking', 'blessing', 'breaking' and 'giving' is important and deserves to be quoted at some length (the italics are Crossan's, not mine):

They indicate, first of all, a process of *equal sharing* whereby whatever food is there is distributed alike to all. [Crossan has explained that in the world outside Jesus' circle a host would sometimes offer inferior food and wine to those he considered of lower status.] But they also indicate something even more important. The first two verbs, *took* and *blessed*, and especially the second, are the actions of the master; the last two, *broke* and *gave*, and especially the second, are the actions of the servant.

Jesus, as master and host, performs instead the role of servant, and all share the same food as equals. There is, however, one further step to be taken. Most of Jesus' first followers would know about but seldom have experienced being served at table by slaves. The male followers would think more experientially of females as preparers and servers of the family food. Jesus took on himself the role not only of servant but of female . . . Far from reclining and being served, Jesus himself serves the meal, serves, like any housewife, the same meal to all including himself.   (*The Historical Jesus*, p. 404)

Now at last we can understand the Emmaus story, and why Cleopas and his wife suddenly realize who Jesus is as the meal begins. For Jesus' behaviour is very curious, and might at first seem downright insulting. He takes over the roles of host and hostess. He takes the bread and blesses it. That is Cleopas' job. Then he breaks it and gives it to them. That is the job of his wife. At the very end of the story, once the two disciples have gone back to Jerusalem, they tell the others that Jesus was revealed to them 'in the breaking of the bread'. Why, of the four actions, do they single that one out? Because that is the point where Jesus begins to do the housewife's job. That is the moment when he departs so very far from convention, and does exactly what he has been used to doing in all the time he has been with his disciples and what, no doubt, Cleopas and his wife have witnessed countless times. The breaking of bread is typical of Jesus, as it was typical of no other man. It can be no one else! Then, of course, they can understand the apparent rudeness of his taking over the roles of host and hostess. Those are precisely the ones they have seen him perform day in, day out. They are his trademark, the trademark of the kingdom of God. It is how God behaves and treats his guests, or rather treats his children.

Meals of this kind, where all are welcomed without distinction and without regard for rank, status, gender or origin, where all have the same food, and the tasks of taking, blessing, breaking and distributing are shared among them, will become the mark of the earliest Church: 'Day by day,' Luke will tell us in Acts 2.46, 'as they spent much time together in the temple, they went from house to house to break bread and eat their food together with glad and generous hearts.' And Paul will remind the Christians in Galatia, 'There is no longer Jew or Greek, there is no longer slave or free, there is no longer male and female; for all of you are one in Christ Jesus' (Galatians 3.28). What Luke is telling us in his story of Emmaus, among many other things, is that their meals together were often occasions when the early Christians felt especially close to the risen Christ. It was as if he was there in their midst, breaking the bread as always he had done in Galilee and beyond. It was not just that the meals brought the memories of him flooding back, though no doubt they did exactly that for those who had known him before he died. Somehow, mysteriously, their meals together made him present; they brought the divine into the room, and reminded them of the intimacy and hospitality of God; they could 'see' Jesus again; they could see God.

Returning to the Emmaus story and reaching its final verses, we realize that night will have fallen. Yet Cleopas and his wife cannot wait till the morning. They rush back to Jerusalem to tell the others. There they find that Jesus has appeared to Simon Peter, also. Luke tells us no more about that encounter. To find a story devoted to an appearance to Peter, we have to turn to John. And yet its significance is not lost on us: it has reunited the community. Now, when Cleopas and his wife burst in on them with their news, they do not dismiss them as fools, but respond with, 'It is true! The Lord has risen!' Not only are Cleopas and his wife back among them, restored to the fold, but all the disciples, it seems, have now found the truth.

As the story ends, however, we are left with one discordant note still ringing, and some uncomfortable questions left unresolved. Why were the women not believed in the first place? How deep does the prejudice about women and their experience of God run in this community? Will it come to the surface again and play its ugly part in shaping the Church? Will the tables that Jesus overturned, the Jesus who played the part of hostess as well as host, be put back up again?

We all know the answers.

Yet still, even now, we Christians find that the risen Christ, the crucified and wounded God, joins us on our journeys, keeps us company, enquires of us, brings to light our manifold stupidities, makes things plain that we have not seen before, accepts our hospitality, eats with us, and in the most ordinary fare gives us a taste of heaven.

A piece of broiled fish

One scene sets up another. Just as Luke's story of the visit of the women to the tomb demanded some resolution, now the stage is set for Jesus to appear to those disciples who have not yet seen him. Luke wastes no time.

> While they were still talking about all this, Jesus himself stood in their midst and said to them, 'Peace be with you!' Terrified and full of fear they thought they were seeing a ghost. He said to them, 'Why are you alarmed? Why do doubts arise in your minds? See my hands and my feet! It is really me! Touch me and see; no ghost has flesh and bones as you see I have.' Saying this, he showed them his hands and his feet. They were still incredulous, with a mixture of joy and astonishment. So he said to them, 'Do you have anything to eat here?' They gave him a piece of broiled fish. He took it and ate it in front of them. (Luke 24.36–43)

Luke has been very careful to join this passage to the Emmaus story: 'While they were still talking about all this,' he begins. And yet in some senses this new story strikes us as very strange. Have not the disciples, including those who were so sceptical at first, just exclaimed, 'It is true! The Lord has risen and has appeared to Simon!'? What has happened to them? Are they really so fickle? And are we to think of Mary of Magdala, Joanna, Mary the mother of James, and the other women who went to the tomb, as 'terrified and full of fear' as the rest? Are Simon Peter, and Cleopas and his wife, full of doubt, thinking Jesus is a ghost? In fact, this passage does not make sense as a sequel to the Emmaus story. It takes us backwards, not forwards in the formation of the community of disciples.

There is another more fundamental respect in which it does not successfully follow on from Emmaus. That was a masterpiece. This is the weakest of all the resurrection stories in all the Gospels. The reason for its failure is plain to see. It is deliberately constructed to argue a single point, to assert that the risen Jesus is not a ghost. It reminds us of the Markan and Matthean versions of the story of the walking on the water, where the figure of Jesus striding across the sea in the dark also make the disciples think they are seeing a ghost and fills them with terror (see Mark 6. 45–52; Matthew 14.22–27 – the story is not in Luke, and John's version makes no mention of a ghost). But those passages have much dramatic power, and leave the mystery of the divine intact. Luke's story here does away with mystery, and shatters all sense of the divine in the process. We have already spoken of the great skill needed when using human language of God, and the fine line that runs between the sublime and the ridiculous. Luke has crossed that line here with particularly heavy feet. No doubt there were those inside or outside the Church of his day who reacted to stories of Jesus' resurrection by asking whether the first disciples did not just see a ghost. We can understand his concern to counter that idea, for indeed it cuts all reality, all meaning out of the resurrection. Alas, unlike his other resurrection stories, this one does nothing to restore either meaning or reality.

It is the piece of broiled fish, of course, which brings the passage crashing down to earth. Genesis 18.8 shows how it should be done: 'And Abraham fetched curds and milk and the calf that had been prepared and he set these before them, he standing over them under the tree, and they ate.' The differences between the two passages might at first seem very slight, for both passages give the menu, and both, in effect, have God eating. Yet while Genesis is genius, Luke's passage is bathos. There is all the difference in the world between Genesis 18.8 and Luke's 'They gave him a piece of broiled fish.

He took it and ate it in front of them.' The first is a bold and profound expression of the intimacy of God, and his enjoyment of our hospitality. The second is simply an unfortunate attempt to argue a point, and is best forgotten.

Another clue to the difference between Genesis 18 and this passage in Luke is that one concerns a meal, while the other is about a mere demonstration. The disciples in Luke do not sit down to eat with Jesus. There has been no invitation to a meal, nor any preparation of one. Jesus simply asks them, if you like, whether they have anything in the fridge, and not because he is hungry, but because he has something to prove. This further separates the broiled fish passage from the story of Emmaus, also. Genesis 18 and Emmaus are all about meeting, about hospitality and the huge significance of the meal. They are about finding God, and finding him in the ordinary, the everyday. Luke 24.36–43 is about none of those things. It fails to point us towards anything of lasting significance.

Mercifully, it is not Luke's last word. That we will come to in the next chapter. But first we must move on to John, who will remind us, as Luke himself did so magnificently at Emmaus, just how a meal story should be told.

'Come and have breakfast'

The Gospel of John is brought to a conclusion at the end of chapter 20, in verses 30–31. That ending allows Thomas' 'My Lord and my God!' to stand as the climax to the whole Gospel. 'Follow that!' we might say. Yet John, or perhaps a second author, does follow it, and with a whole chapter. We will briefly revisit John 20 in the next chapter of this book, but for now it is to this added chapter that we must turn.

It is not for us to enter into the long-running discussion about the authorship of this chapter, and whether it was written by the same person as the rest of the Gospel. Opinions among scholars remain divided. If it was written by the same hand (and there is a fair amount of evidence to encourage that belief), then why did the author conclude his Gospel at 20.30–31, only to reopen it and have to provide a second conclusion at 21.24–25? That is a question which invites some enjoyable speculation, but which cannot be answered with any certainty. For our purposes it matters not. What we are interested in is power of storytelling, and the handling of the mystery of the resurrection and the wounded God. We shall continue to call the author of the chapter 'John', while being aware that that is shorthand for 'John, or a close associate of John's'.

Even those who would wish to stress that John did write it often suggest that this chapter comes as an anticlimax after the appearances to Mary of Magdala and Thomas. Undoubtedly, the story of Mary is the finest of all the resurrection stories in John and, indeed, we would say in any of the Gospels, and we have already explored the key role played by the Thomas passage. In certain respects John 21 will take us a step or two backwards, instead of moving the narrative on. Nevertheless, 'anticlimax' does not well prepare us for what is in store in John 21, for that contains two episodes of great power. The second of them we will leave to our next chapter. The first we will explore now.

After these things Jesus revealed himself to the disciples beside the Sea of Tiberias. He revealed himself in this way. Gathered together were Simon Peter and Thomas called the Twin, Nathanael (the one from Cana in Galilee), the sons of Zebedee and two others from among his disciples. Simon Peter said to them, 'I'm going fishing.' 'We're coming with you,' they replied. So they went off and got into the boat. That night they caught nothing. When dawn was breaking Jesus stood on the shore. None of the disciples knew it was Jesus. Jesus called to them, 'Lads, you haven't caught anything to eat, have you?' 'No,' they answered. He said to them, 'Throw the net to the right side of the boat, and you'll find something.' So they threw it, and the number of fish was so great, they did not have the strength to haul it in. Then that disciple whom Jesus loved said to Peter, 'It is the Lord!' Once he heard it was the Lord, Peter tucked in his outer garment (for otherwise he was naked) and jumped into the sea. The other disciples continued to come in by boat, towing the net full of fish, for they were not far from the shore – only about a hundred yards off.

When they landed, they saw a charcoal fire, with a fish laid on it, and some bread. Jesus said to them, 'Bring some of the fish you have caught.' So Simon Peter went on board and dragged the net ashore loaded with large fish, one hundred and fifty-three of them. Although there were so many, the net was not broken.

Jesus said to them, 'Come and have breakfast.'

None of the disciples dared enquire, 'Who are you?' They knew it was the Lord. Jesus came over, took the bread and gave it to them, and did the same with the fish. (Now this was the third time that Jesus revealed himself to the disciples after he was raised from the dead.)   (John 21.1–14)

Luke has a story remarkably like this one, not in his small series of resurrection stories, but much earlier in his Gospel, at 5.1–11. There it describes the call of the first disciples. It begins with Jesus standing beside the Sea of Galilee, surrounded by a crowd hungry for his teaching. Two fishing boats are there, with the fishermen washing their nets. One of them belongs to Simon Peter, and Jesus gets into it, asks him to row a little way out from the shore, and then proceeds to teach the people from the boat. When he is finished, he tells Simon to put out into the deep water and let down his nets. Peter tells him they have worked all night and caught nothing, but he follows Jesus' instructions nevertheless. So many fish are then caught that the nets begin to break, and they have to signal to the fishermen in the other boat to come and help them. They tip the catch into the boats, which are then so heavily laden they begin to sink. Simon cries, 'Go away from me, Lord, for I am a sinful man!' But Jesus reassures him with the words, 'Do not be afraid. From now on you will be catching people.' Luke tells us that James and John are there as Simon's partners, and concludes the story by saying, 'When they had brought the boats to the shore, they left everything and followed him.'

The similarities are, of course, very striking, yet so are the differences. Beyond the incidental details, the new context provided by John is of huge significance, and his story, unlike Luke's, is about a meal.

The story begins with a disappointment. Where is Mary of Magdala? It is perfectly possible to include her, and the other women disciples, among 'the disciples' to whom Jesus appears in 20.19, the passage that leads into the appearance to Thomas. Indeed, it would be quite wrong to exclude them. But here, beside the Sea of Galilee, there are only seven disciples, five of them named, and those are all men, and they are going fishing. One of the unnamed disciples turns out to be 'that disciple whom Jesus loved', and Richard Bauckham suggests that 'nothing prevents' us from thinking of the other one as a woman. 'In a realistic story of fishing the disciples have to be men,' he continues, 'but in their representative role they can stand also for women' (*Gospel Women*, p. 285). He has just reminded us that the number seven symbolizes completeness, and argued that therefore these fishermen are 'representative of all disciples'. His discussion has some force, but the fact remains that John has set this story in an exclusively male world. Whatever Bauckham might say, the focus is on the men. In a real sense, as he admits, the women are not there, nor will they reappear in the rest of John's final chapter. We have another example here of what we have grown used to, alas, in the Bible, whether in the Hebrew or the Christian Scriptures: if they are lucky women are given a scene where they are centre stage, two if they are very fortunate; then they exit left and the men take over and continue to dominate the action. (The Song of Songs, and the books of Ruth and Esther provide glorious exceptions to this general rule, but they are the only ones, and there are none at all in the New Testament.) Unless we are entirely honest about the bias of our Scriptures, we will not be able to face the extent of the similar bias that still exists within the Church.

What does the return of these male disciples to Galilee and to their fishing on the Sea of Tiberias signify? Is it a case of 'aimless activity undertaken in desperation', as Raymond Brown would suggest (*The Gospel According to John*, vol. 2,

XIII–XXI, p. 1096)? Is Peter in particular in a state of denial, as Mark Stibbe argues (*John*, 1993, p. 210)? After Jesus' appearances in John 20 the scene must certainly come as a surprise. We have already mentioned that, in the passage immediately preceding the appearance to Thomas, Jesus commissions his disciples to continue his work, and gives them the gift of the Holy Spirit to enable them to do so. So what are they doing here in Galilee, back in their old haunts, at their old pursuits? When we recall the version of the story in Luke 5, we cannot help wondering whether they have not gone right back to the beginning. In both Mark's and Matthew's resurrection stories the disciples are told to return to Galilee. 'He is going ahead of you to Galilee,' the angel tells the women at the tomb in Mark 16.7 and Matthew 28.7, 'there you will see him' (the Greek is the same in each case). But there has been no such instruction or prediction in John. It is almost as if John 20 has never been told, as if the disciples are back where they started.

But of course they are not. Though the particular stories of John 20 seem hidden in the shadows of the new narrative, the disciples do not react as if this is the very first time they have seen the risen Jesus (and, of course, the end of the passage says it is not); and by placing this passage where he does in his Gospel, John encourages us to make links with other stories that have gone before, especially the feeding of the five thousand, and Peter's denial of Jesus in the courtyard of the high priest's house.

A night's fishing yields nothing. 'Ah well,' we might say, 'there will always be another night.' But such a remark would be too casual by far. These men are fishing in order to *eat*. Luke's story of the miracle of the huge catch is set against the background of the local fishing industry. When we first see the fishermen, they are washing their nets, and later in the story there is cooperation between two crews to help land the catch. Simon Peter, James and John and the others are clearly fishing to sell at the local market, and so feed their families. A night's fishing without any success is a serious matter, particularly given the taxes they already have to pay to the Roman authorities. Nevertheless, the consequences are more stark in

John. 'Lads, you haven't caught anything to eat, have you?' Jesus asks them. He knows the answer. They have nothing. They will go hungry that day. Their poverty reminds us all too clearly of the five thousand, who also gather beside the Sea of Galilee, and have nothing between them, except one small boy's five barley loaves and two fish.

Almost everything the feeding of the five thousand meant then, the miraculous catch of fish and the meal Jesus prepares mean here. Ever since Jerome, who wrote in the fourth century and early fifth, there have been endless discussions of the significance of the particular number of fish caught. After the dust of those arguments has settled, only one thing about the number remains clear: it is *big*. At first the disciples find the net so heavy with fish that they cannot haul it in to the side of the boat and, when later Peter drags it ashore all on his own, we catch a whiff of Hercules' aftershave in the Galilee air. So there is *abundance* here, just as there was in the other miracle beside the sea, when the people had more than they could eat and the disciples had to pick up the remains. The seven disciples have far more than they need. So this story becomes another about the prodigality of God, his sheer, absurd-seeming, all-caution-thrown-to-the-winds generosity. Earlier in his Gospel, John has Jesus saying, 'I came that they might have life, and have it abundantly' (10.10). Exactly so. Here is the risen Jesus providing 153 fish, plus one that has been mysteriously caught already, for seven men's breakfast! It is ridiculous. It is wonderful.

Yet the meal he has prepared is really for just one of the seven, Simon Peter. That will become even clearer in the next passage, when after the meal is over Jesus will enter into dialogue with him. But it is already apparent in the verses we have quoted. The disciple Jesus loves plays his part, and once again, as he did beside the empty tomb, is the first to perceive the truth that lies behind what eyes can see. Yet after he has recognized Jesus and told Peter, he retreats back into the little company of the seven. It is Peter and Peter alone who tucks up his robe and jumps into the sea to swim ashore, and it is Peter who drags the net to the land.

The details of the hour and the charcoal fire reveal Jesus' intentions. We have heard of such a fire before in John's Gospel, just once, in 18.18. There Jesus has been arrested and taken to the house of the high priest for questioning. Peter is standing in the courtyard of the house when the servant girl guarding the gate says to him, 'Aren't you also one of this man's disciples?' 'No I am not!' he replies. Then John continues, 'Now the slaves and the temple police had made a charcoal fire, because it was cold, and they were standing around warming themselves. So Peter stood with them and warmed himself.' Three times Peter denies any knowledge of Jesus, and at the moment of his third denial the cock crows to mark the start of a new day. And now Jesus is standing on the shore of the Sea of Galilee as dawn is breaking.

So this breakfast is meant to remind us of the moment when Peter denies he knows Jesus. It is designed to take us back to Peter's lowest point in the whole story, and face us with its horror. Does Jesus mean to drown Peter in his shame? That will only become clear in the next passage, which we will come to at the end of our next chapter. But we can say now that the answer to the question is a resounding no, and that, for the present, will suffice.

This passage contains none of the bathos of Luke's piece about the broiled fish. Indeed, Jesus' invitation, 'Come and have breakfast', is surely one of the great lines of the Bible. Sometimes the Bible's storytellers and poets manage to capture something indescribably precious of the mystery and the wonder of God in a tiny handful of words, and express what no theological treatise could ever convey, however many volumes long. 'And the Lord would speak to Moses face to face, as one speaks to a friend' in Exodus 33.11 is one example, and Exodus 32.11 provides another with its, 'And Moses soothed the face of the Lord his God.' 'Come and have breakfast', just two words in John's original Greek, is another. It bears the warmth of God's eternal, yet ever-fresh hospitality. The invitation is not issued to those who are worthy to receive it (as if anyone could be). It is given to a man who carries the guilt and the shame of threefold denial. It captures, also, God's simplicity and his desire that we cooperate with him to feed the world's hungers. He supplies no extravagant feast, just a single fish, and invites his friends to add fish of their own to make a proper job of it.

This resurrection meal beside the lake lacks one thing present in the story of the feeding of the five thousand: the crowd. Like the Last Supper, it is prepared for a few, and they are the initiated, people already belonging to Jesus' circle. It misses as a result a vital dimension of the divine, boundless and entirely unconditional generosity. Yet no one story, however brilliant, can contain everything. It still remains the case, that in this little circle gathered round the charcoal fire beside the Sea of Galilee, we see the greatness and the strangeness of the kingdom of God, a kingdom like no other that has ever been.

4

Commissioning and empowerment

———◆———

Putting Jesus back in the crowd

Despite all the differences between the Gospels, in the resurrection stories of Matthew, Luke and John there is a single movement in the overall plot, from the shock of the discovery of the empty tomb, to encounter with the risen Jesus, to Jesus' sending out his disciples to carry on his work. Only in Mark is the plot cut short, but that is because his narrative ends so abruptly.

In Mark's and Matthew's stories of the empty tomb, the angel instructs the women to tell the other disciples what they have found, and in Matthew that instruction is repeated by the risen Jesus when he meets them on the road. Similarly in John, Jesus tells Mary of Magdala to go back to the others with the news of their encounter. In Luke, the women are not given any explicit instruction, but then they do not need one; they go straight from the tomb to tell their fellow disciples. In the Emmaus story, Cleopas and his wife are so keen to tell their news, that as soon as Jesus has left them, they walk (or run?) the seven miles back to Jerusalem in the dark.

So far only those who were with Jesus in Galilee, and who have journeyed with him to Jerusalem and his death, have discovered the mystery of the resurrection. We might suppose that is inevitable, but it is not. Mark, Matthew and Luke all talk of the afternoon sun being turned to night for three hours at the crucifixion. Matthew speaks of an earthquake shaking Jerusalem, of *two* earthquakes, one at the moment of Jesus' death, the other when the angel descends upon his tomb. He speaks of Jewish soldiers caught up in the events at the tomb. Conceivably, the resurrection could have been an event that was truly overwhelming in its scale and impact. The people of Jerusalem, including Pilate and the high priest, might have seen 'the Son of Man coming in clouds with great power and glory', with the sun again darkened, the moon refusing to shine, the stars falling from the heavens, and the powers in the heavens shaken to their foundations (see Mark 13.26 and 24–25). But then it would not have been the resurrection of Jesus of Nazareth. For he refuses at the outset to make any attempt to take the world by storm, as we see clearly from the stories of the temptations in the wilderness (Mark 1.12–13; Matthew 4.1–11; Luke 4.1–13). Nor would it have been the appearance of the wounded God.

Except for the touches of melodrama in Matthew's story of the empty tomb, things in the Gospels are done on the quiet. And the news of the tomb, or even of encounters with Jesus himself, is at first shared only among the disciples. But we must beware lest, in our mind's eye, we make that group too small. There is a famous passage in Paul's First Letter to the Corinthians which runs like this:

> I handed on to you as of first importance what I in turn had received: that Christ died for our sins according to the scriptures, and that he was buried, and that he was raised on the third day according to the scriptures, and that he appeared to Cephas [the Aramaic form of the name Peter; both words mean 'rock'], then to the twelve. Then he appeared to over five hundred brothers and sisters at one time, most of whom are still alive, though some have died. Then he appeared to James [that is Jesus' brother, who became a leader of the Church in Jerusalem] then to all the apostles. Last of all, as to one untimely born, he appeared to me.
>
> (1 Corinthians 15.3–8)

This is an intriguing passage because, of course, it seems to tell a rather different story from any of the Gospels. Paul makes no mention of specific appearances to the women, though naturally we should include the women disciples (and possibly children?) among the 500, while none of the Gospels speaks of an appearance to Jesus' brother James, and indeed

James does not appear in the narrative at all until we reach the book of Acts. N. T. Wright discusses this and other passages in Paul at very great length in Part II of his *The Resurrection of the Son of God*. It is not for us to enter into the discussion, but as we prepare to return to the Gospels, we should take note of one very striking detail of Paul's account: the size of the group to which Jesus appears after Peter and the Twelve. More than 500 people is a lot.

We are used to thinking of Jesus as having had a very small inner circle. Every time I approach the high altar in Chester Cathedral, where I work, I see Jesus surrounded by 12 men. The reredos is a nineteenth-century mosaic depicting the Last Supper, and of course it is beautifully done, and of course it has an obvious appropriateness about it, and of course it is faithful to the Gospel accounts of that meal, but it irritates me and I wish it were not there. It is not the artist's fault. It is rather the fault of the Gospels, which make the women disciples almost completely invisible, until the stories of the crucifixion and resurrection, and the fault of the Church whose male leaders through the centuries have been so keen to maintain that bias and have used their authority to enforce it. At least the women do feature in many of the resurrection stories, but we can still be forgiven for imagining just a small band of people being involved, and not merely at the empty tomb. In the passage in Matthew we are about to explore, where Jesus commissions his disciples, only the Eleven are there. The appearance at Emmaus is to but two people, and the one we are yet to examine in John 20.19–23 has the disciples together in one room behind locked doors. There are only seven invited to breakfast beside the Sea of Galilee, and the passage beyond that will narrow the focus right down to Jesus and two others, really to just Jesus and Peter.

Luke, however, in the end leaves the doors wide open, and would seem to have in mind a much larger group. The beginning of his book of Acts will pick up exactly where his Gospel leaves off. In Acts 1.12–14 Luke refers to the disciples returning from the Mount of Olives, from where Jesus has been lifted up, and going to 'the room upstairs where they were staying'. He then speaks of the Eleven being there, with 'some women and with Mary, Jesus' mother, and his brothers'. His inclusion of Mary of Nazareth and her other sons in this list comes as a complete surprise. Nothing in the Gospel since the stories of the birth of Jesus in Luke 1—2 has prepared us for it. Yet there they are, and this might well suggest we should include them among the disciples gathered at the end of his Gospel. Either that, or else we have to envisage them popping up out of nowhere to join the disciples during the period of 40 days which in Acts 1.3 precedes the ascension.

In the light of 1 Corinthians 15, Acts 1.15 is equally interesting. 'In those days Peter stood up in the midst of the brothers and sisters (together the crowd numbered about one hundred and twenty people).' It is a tight-knit group, for the Greek word Luke uses for 'people' makes clear their names are all known, even if he does not report them. It is not entirely clear how this much larger group relates to the one of the previous few verses, or to the group in Luke 24.33ff. But a good story-teller does not give us all the information at once, but lets details emerge as the narrative proceeds. We are used to that technique from the Gospels, and will soon find an example of it, when we turn to Matthew. If that is what Luke is doing here, then we have to envisage all those 120 people being present when Jesus comes to stand among his disciples in 24.33ff.

Where in the story of the beginnings of the Church we should place that even more remarkable appearance to over 500 people is by no means clear, and I will not even attempt a suggestion. But we must allow Luke and Paul to remind us how partial that scene is in Chester Cathedral, and all the other images like it. After all, the Gospels repeatedly talk of crowds of people flocking to hear Jesus teach, and finding healing. A great crowd surrounds him with their acclamations as he rides into Jerusalem, also, and let us not be quick to identify them, as some of our liturgical texts do, with that other crowd, manipulated by the authorities, which soon we hear baying for his blood. As early as the start of Luke 10 we hear of Jesus sending out 70 or 72 followers of his to prepare the ground for him as he travels south towards Jerusalem. So let us put Jesus back in the crowd, and the risen Jesus in particular. 'Then he appeared to over five hundred brothers and sisters at one time'; 'Together the crowd numbered about one hundred and twenty people.' Let us not forget that, though Matthew and John will take us back to a much smaller stage.

'I am with you always'

The final passage of Matthew's Gospel reads like this:

> The eleven disciples went to Galilee, to the mountain to which Jesus had directed them. When they saw him, they worshipped him; but some wavered. Jesus came and said to them, 'All authority in heaven and on earth has been given to me. Go therefore and turn all peoples into disciples, baptizing them in the name of the Father and of the Son and of the Holy Spirit, and teaching them to heed everything that I have commanded you. And behold, I am with you always, to the end of the age.'
>
> (Matthew 28.16–20)

So only the Eleven are there, the Twelve minus Judas Iscariot who has betrayed Jesus to the authorities and has since committed suicide. Their status is immeasurably enhanced by the other disciples being excluded, and it is easy to see this passage as designed, in part, to achieve that end, and as reflecting struggles for power and authority within the early Church.

Yet let us not get carried away by the language of these verses, or give them too strident a tone. Matthew's is, after all, the Gospel that contains the Sermon on the Mount.

This final scene is set on a mountain. There was no mention of that earlier. The women were simply to tell the disciples to 'go to Galilee'. But, that is not an unfortunate discrepancy, just an example of Matthew the storyteller not having told us everything at once. The setting reminds us of Sinai, and also of Mount Nebo in Deuteronomy 34, the mountain that Moses climbs, to be given the sight of the Promised Land just before he dies. Nebo signifies the handing over of the work of Moses to Joshua, so that he can bring it to completion and lead the people across the Jordan, into the Land. So here Jesus hands on the leadership in the great task of building the kingdom of God, or 'the kingdom of heaven', as

Matthew prefers, to the Eleven. There, however, the comparison with Nebo ends. Here in Matthew 28 there is no death, but only God.

Though some hesitate, the worship of Jesus is entirely appropriate. It is what the magi do near the beginning of the Gospel (2.11), or later the leper who comes for healing in 8.2, or the synagogue ruler, whose daughter is so desperately ill (9.18), the disciples themselves, when Jesus has reached them by walking on the sea (14.33), or the Canaanite woman who comes to plead for her daughter too (15.25); it is what the women of the empty tomb have already done, in their encounter with Jesus (28.9). In all those cases the Greek verb used is the same. Like Moses on Sinai, or Peter, James and John on the Mount of Transfiguration, the Eleven are in the heart of the divine.

There is another mountain we should recall, beyond Sinai or Nebo. Before he begins his work in Galilee and calls his first disciples, Jesus in Matthew is taken by the devil 'to a very high mountain' and is there shown 'all the kingdoms of the world and their splendour'. 'All these I will give you,' says the devil, 'if you fall down and worship me.' Jesus sends him packing in no uncertain terms (Matthew 4.8–10). It is a vital moment in the unfolding of the story. Jesus is at a crossroads. One path leads to Rome, the other to Golgotha. One means the ruthless exercising of power and authority of a Roman emperor, or of a Herod like the one who slaughters all the babies and infants in and around Bethlehem, lest his position be challenged (Matthew 2.16–18). The other road will take Jesus to another mountain where he will sit and teach the people to refuse to take vengeance, to respond to a slap on the face that is designed to humiliate and enforce submission, by quietly but defiantly turning the other cheek (5.38–39); to love their enemies and pray for their persecutors (5.43–45); to 'strive first for the kingdom of *God* and his righteousness' (6.33) and to pray, 'Our Father in heaven, hallowed be *your* name' (6.9); not to pass judgement on others, to start taking the specks out of other people's eyes when they have great logs in their own (7.1–4)! On another occasion, as he travels that same road, his disciples will ask him a question that comes straight from the world of Rome or the Herodian palaces: 'Who is the greatest in the kingdom of heaven?' His answer will be most remarkable. He will call a small child and put him or her in the middle of his circle: 'I solemnly tell you,' he will say, 'unless you turn and become like children, you will never enter the kingdom of heaven' (18.1–3). He will do that, not because the children of his day are so sweet and innocent, but because they are so far from the normal centres of power, because they have no power, no honour, no authority, no significance in those places where 'significant' things are decided or performed, because they are so vulnerable; because, in short, the kingdom of heaven means the turning of the kingdom of Rome on its head. When he reaches the centre of power in Jerusalem, the precincts of the temple, the children will be there with him, crying 'Hosanna to the Son of David!' (21.15). They will be shouting for his coronation, but the temple authorities, together with the Romans, will see instead to his crucifixion. It will not be the ceremony the children had in mind. Yet when he dies, the curtain of the temple will be split from top to bottom, and at last, at long last, God will walk free.

We must remember all this and more as we now hear those words, 'All authority in heaven and earth has been given to me', and as we hear the commission, 'Go therefore and turn all peoples into disciples.' Too often we Christians have forgotten that the voice that utters them is the same as recites the beatitudes 23 chapters earlier. Far too often, we have taken Jesus' words as a clear invitation to gallop on our chargers towards the conventional corridors of power. But the kingdom of God is not like any other, and a wounded God does not gallop anywhere.

The movement begun by John the Baptist came to an end or was absorbed into the Church, because John did not teach his followers to baptize. *He* was the Baptizer, not them. So when he was put to death, it was only a matter of time before his movement ceased also. Not so with Jesus of Nazareth. Carefully he prepared his followers for the work of establishing that strange and wonderful kingdom of God. When he died, it was a beginning, not an end. In this final passage in

Matthew he formally commissions his disciples, as once God commissioned the prophets, to continue where he has left off, and to take to all the nations of the world what he has been trailing round the towns and villages of Galilee.

He promises that he will be with them always. That is more God-talk, as we realize if we recall God's promise to Jacob in Genesis 28.15, to Joshua in Deuteronomy 31.23, or to his people in Isaiah 41.10 and 43.5 or Ezekiel 34.30. Very near the beginning of his Gospel, Matthew quotes Isaiah 7.14: 'Behold, the virgin shall conceive and bear a son, and they shall call his name Emmanuel,' which means, 'God with us!' (Matthew 1.23).

Thus he begins his Gospel with the cry, 'God with us!' and ends with the calm reassurance of the God who has been through crucifixion, 'I am with you always.'

It is very nearly all we need to know.

'Repentance for the forgiveness of sins'

We have already explored the first part of the passage in Luke where Jesus appears to the larger group of his disciples (the incident of the broiled fish), and we have also established that Luke invites us to imagine a very large group being present, around 120 people, a group that includes both the women who were at the empty tomb, and Mary of Nazareth, Jesus' mother, and his brothers. This is how the passage proceeds, and how Luke concludes his Gospel:

> Then Jesus said to them, 'This is what my words meant which I spoke to you while I was still with you: all that was written about me in the Law of Moses, in the Prophets, and in the Psalms must be fulfilled.' Then he opened their minds to understand the Scriptures. 'Thus it stands written,' he said: 'the Messiah is to suffer and rise from the dead on the third day, and in his name repentance for the forgiveness of sins is to be preached to all the nations, beginning from Jerusalem. You are witnesses of this! Now see, I am sending upon you what my Father promised. You are to remain here in the city until you are clothed with power from on high.'

Then Jesus led them out as far as Bethany and, lifting up his hands, he blessed them. While he was blessing them he was parted from them and was carried up to heaven. And they worshipped him and returned to Jerusalem with great joy, and spent their time in the temple, constantly praising God. (24.44–53)

When the passage begins, we are still very close to the resurrection and to the moment of its discovery. Cleopas and his wife have set out for Emmaus in the afternoon of what we now call Easter Day; their evening meal has been prepared, and they have then come the seven miles back to Jerusalem to tell the others what happened, so several more hours have elapsed; but verse 36 tells us, 'While they were still talking about all this, Jesus himself stood in their midst.' So it is the night after Easter.

Acts would suggest, however, a considerable gap between the appearance at the beginning of the passage and the episode at Bethany at the end. For Acts 1.6–11 gives its own version of the ascension story, and prefaces it with, 'After his suffering he presented himself alive to them by many convincing proofs, appearing to them for a period of forty days and speaking about the kingdom of God' (Acts 1.3). It is this verse (and this verse alone) that has determined the Church's liturgical calendar, and its placing Ascension Day 40 days after Easter. Are we meant to slip those 40 days into the Gospel, between Jesus telling his disciples to remain in Jerusalem and his leading them out to Bethany? Given the technique of biblical storytellers of saving up details and putting them into the narrative at a later point, the answer is probably yes.

Jesus' reinterpretation of the Scriptures reminds us at once of the dialogue on the road to Emmaus. But there he was simply (!) showing Cleopas and his wife how the Scriptures had long spoken of his coming and of his death and resurrection. Now, with the other disciples present, he introduces a new subject to his exposition: the task they are now faced with of preaching 'repentance for the forgiveness of sins to all the nations, beginning from Jerusalem'. That too, he claims, belongs to the pattern of the Scriptures.

That exact phrase, 'repentance for the forgiveness of sins' occurs very near the start of the Gospel, not in the preaching of Jesus, but in that of John the Baptist (Luke 3.3). Yet now, after all that Jesus has taught, after the establishment of his new family, after his death and the triumph it represents, after the resurrection itself, then the nature and extent of the 'repentance' that is required is fully known. John the Baptist's vision was radical enough, but Jesus' meant the overturning of almost all of the social, political and economic conventions of his day. Still, of course, it presents an extremely radical challenge to so many of the prevailing attitudes and practices of the society in which we live, wherever in the world that may be. Repentance means the rising to that challenge, both in our private living and in our public conduct, as individuals and as a Church.

And such repentance leads inexorably to forgiveness. This Jesus, who has been arrested for making the mercy of God so freely available, and for protesting against all attempts to keep it in one place and in the hands of a few powerful men for their gracious dispensing; who has been treated with contempt, mocked and finally put to death by the most painful and humiliating death the Romans knew; who still bears the marks of the nails in his hands and feet, this Jesus still comes trailing forgiveness! He does not call for revenge. Instead he packs his disciples' rucksacks full of the mercy of God.

Yet is the Jesus of this passage quite radical enough? Is the Parable of the Father and the Two Lost Sons included in the disciples' baggage? It seems not, for that parable, found only in Luke (15.11–32), puts forgiveness first, and repentance a clear second. Both sons grievously humiliate the father of the parable. The first asks for his inheritance while his father is still alive, and then turns it into cash, leaves for Gentile territory, and squanders every penny he has. The elder son fails to play the part of go-between at that point, and later refuses to welcome his brother home and play his role in helping his father entertain the guests in the feast he has organized. In a society that placed such a high value on male honour, and so much stress on the authority of a father over his children, the actions of both sons are extremely serious. 'Honour your father and your mother,' say both versions of the Ten Commandments (Exodus 20.12; Deuteronomy 5.16). 'Whoever strikes father or mother,' says Exodus 21.15, 'shall be put to death.'

Yet how does the father of the parable act towards his two lost sons (for surely the elder son is lost to him, also; does not this son accuse him of treating him like a slave? – Luke 15.29)? When the younger one returns, his father throws all caution, all concern for honour and dignity to the four winds, runs up the road to meet him, flings his arms around him and smothers him with kisses. In doing all that he acts like a mother, but then he resumes the role of father by giving orders for his own best robe and signet ring, signs of his authority in the family and the village, to be put on his son, for sandals to be put on his feet to demonstrate that he is his son and not his slave, and for the fatted calf to be killed and a great party to be held. And some of this he does *before* his son repents. Certainly, the son has prepared a speech for his return. Quite reasonably afraid of how he will be received, he works out what to say: 'Father, I have sinned against heaven and before you; I am no longer worthy to be called your son.' But at that point in the story, he is only bent on saving his skin. It is a calculated, political speech, containing no true repentance. In any case, the father does not allow him to give it, not until they have embraced. *Then* the son blurts it out, and *then* he means it. His father's forgiveness brings him to repentance. And that repentance means he can enjoy the forgiveness to the full extent, best robe, ring, sandals, fatted calf, feasting, dancing, the lot.

The father's treatment of his elder son is equally unexpected, and just as magnanimous. When this son finds out his brother has returned and his father has given a feast in his honour, he refuses to have any part in it. So once again the father throws away all concern for his honour and dignity and goes outside, as a mother would, to plead with him. The son releases upon him the full extent of his anger, and accuses him of rank favouritism. To be fair to this son, that is exactly what his father's treatment of his brother looks like. But the father does not say, as well he might have done, 'How dare you speak to me like that! Get inside and do your duty and embrace your brother – it matters not what you feel – and help me entertain my guests!' The first hearers of the parable would surely have expected the father to say that, or something like it. But instead he calls him *teknon*. That Greek word is virtually untranslatable in the context. It does not mean simply 'son'. It is the common word for child, yet this son is a grown man, and the father means no humiliation, but only affection, for that is what *teknon* is filled with. It is the term a mother might use in the circumstances. But once again this father resumes his male role: '*Teknon*,' he says, 'you are always with me, and *everything I have is yours*.' This father does not love one son at the expense of the other. The parable ends with the elder son's status in the family being plainly and strongly reasserted. Whether this act of forgiveness, nearly as astonishing as the first, produces repentance, we are not told. The story finishes there, not because the ending is missing, but because we, the hearers of the story, have to respond for ourselves. Will we answer that freely offered forgiveness of God with our own repentance, so that we can join the celebrations?

Many people believe that parable gets us closer than any other to the heart of Jesus' teaching and of his vision of God, and provides a clue to his treatment of those he encountered. I am one of them. Yet it is so radical, that even in the New Testament we see it largely ignored, and replaced by the established view that repentance must come first before forgiveness can be offered. And of course, the Church went on to preach that old view with all its might and main for centuries, and still does.

So Luke does not get it quite right at the end of his Gospel. He should have it the other way round. He should have the risen Jesus telling his disciples to proclaim 'the forgiveness of sins for repentance'.

Jesus sends them out to 'all the nations'. Luke has been leading up to this point ever since he had Simeon take the infant Jesus in his arms and sing his famous song:

Master, now you are dismissing your slave in peace,
according to your word;
for my eyes have seen your salvation,
which you have prepared in the presence of all
    peoples,
a light for revelation to the Gentiles
and for glory to your people Israel.

(2.29–32)

The whole of the book of Acts will be devoted to the story of
how the disciples fulfil Jesus' vision. Its story begins, as Jesus
says it must, in Jerusalem, and it ends with Paul preaching in
Rome. The news of the strange kingdom of God is brought
to the heart of the Roman empire.

Before they go to Bethany, Jesus promises his disciples that
they will be given the strength, *divine* strength for the task.
They will be 'clothed with power from on high'. They will be
given not the purple robe and laurel wreath of the emperor,
but something far superior: God's best robe, his signet ring,
and new sandals, made in heaven! The moment when they
will get dressed in all that will come in Acts 2.1–4, in Luke's
dramatic story of Pentecost.

And so Jesus leaves them with his blessing. On his deathbed
Isaac blesses his sons Jacob and Esau (Genesis 27); Jacob in
turn blesses his sons before he dies (Genesis 49), and Moses
also pronounces blessing on the people of Israel before his
death (Deuteronomy 33). They are not just bidding farewell,
but passing on their authority and their calling. Jesus is doing
the same for his disciples though, of course, in his case death
has happened already, and been quite undone.

Bethany has featured in Luke's Gospel once already, in
19.29, as the place outside Jerusalem where his triumphal
entry into the city began. So now it marks his triumphal entry
into heaven.

In John, as we have seen, Jesus' being 'lifted up' on the cross,
his being raised from the dead, and his being lifted up to
heaven are all one, but three stages of the one shattering
triumph of divine love. It is undoubtedly the most sophisticated and satisfying of the Gospel portraits of Jesus' exalta-

tion. Luke speaks as if crucifixion, resurrection and ascension were three separate events. And he speaks, also, of Jesus' ascension in terms of parting. The disciples are on their own now, as they wait for God to come and clothe them. By contrast the final appearances to the disciples in John are of the ascended as well as the risen Jesus, for when Mary of Magdala finds him, the final stage of his exaltation is already upon him.

Yet Luke's way of speaking (and that, of course, is what it is) captures some aspects of the truth more firmly than John. The shock of the initial encounters with the risen Jesus receded. The shattering discovery of the wounded God came to take up its position at the heart of Christian preaching. And the experience of those who had followed Jesus from Galilee, who had witnessed, or nearly witnessed Golgotha, and *then* had found him, could not be reduplicated, though it came very close to it in Paul. As he himself claims in 1 Corinthians 15.8, the risen Jesus 'appeared last of all' to him. The presence and the power of Jesus were still keenly felt in the fellowship of the Church, yet now they needed a new language to convey their reality. That became the language of the Spirit.

Luke's talk of distance and presence are, in fact, but two sides of the same coin. For God is both familiar and strange, closer than breathing and still far beyond. The disciples in Luke know that to be true. When Jesus is 'carried up to heaven', they do not fall into a sobbing heap. Quite the contrary. Now at last, they worship him. At last they all recognize the full truth of what Mary of Magdala, Joanna, Mary the mother of James, and the other women found at the tomb. Just at the moment he disappears, the scales finally fall from their eyes, and they can see him for who he is! Was it not the same at Emmaus for Cleopas and his wife? Did not their recognition of Jesus coincide precisely with his disappearing from their sight? God is both familiar and strange, closer than breathing and far beyond. When we ourselves are most keenly aware of the intimacy of God, then we are most overwhelmed by God's mystery. When God seems most 'other', then God comes particularly close. It is a fact of life.

And so the disciples return to the temple. The Gospel of Luke begins there with the priest Zechariah burning incense inside the sanctuary. A little later it speaks of the prophet Anna coming upon the infant Jesus in its precincts. 'She did not leave the temple,' Luke tells us, 'but worshipped there night and day with fasting and prayer' (2.37). Now the disciples spend all their time there, too. The story has come full circle. Only now the temple is different, and the time for fasting is over. The curtain across the Holy of Holies is gone, torn from top to bottom. God at last is free!

No wonder, now they have all finally tumbled to the truth, the disciples are filled with great joy!

'Receive the Holy Spirit'

We have already summarized the passage in John 20 where Jesus appears to the disciples on the evening of Easter Day, but we moved on very quickly to the story that follows it, where Thomas makes his momentous declaration, 'My Lord and my God!' Let us now return to John 20.19–23, and spend more time with it.

Now on the evening of that first day of the week, when, for fear of the Jews the disciples had locked the doors of the place where they were, Jesus came and stood in the midst of them and said, 'Peace be with you.' Having said this, he showed them his hands and his side. When they saw the Lord, the disciples rejoiced. Jesus said to them again, 'Peace be with you. As the Father sent me, so I send you.' Having said this he breathed on them and said, 'Receive the Holy Spirit. If you forgive the sins of any, they are forgiven them, if you hold them, they are held fast.'

This follows on immediately after Jesus' encounter with Mary of Magdala, and her returning to the others with the cry, 'I have seen the Lord!' We see now that, like another John the Baptist, she has prepared the way for Jesus to appear to them.

They do not have to wait long. That very evening Jesus stands in their midst.

He comes to them when they have locked the doors because of their 'fear of the Jews'. The way in which John speaks of 'the Jews' in his Gospel, and the hostility towards them we find expressed elsewhere in the New Testament, have wreaked most terrible havoc down the centuries, in no century more so than in the one that has just gone. We can be sure that if John and the other writers had known how their words would be misused, they would have written differently. Let us recall that Jesus himself was a Jew, all the people in this locked room are Jews, the author of the Gospel was a Jew, and that 'Jews' here is shorthand for 'the Jewish religious authorities'.

The fear of the disciples is realistic enough, however. Jesus threatened the structures, purpose and very meaning of the Jerusalem temple at a fundamental level. That is especially clear in John, where the story of Jesus' 'cleansing' of the temple is set near the beginning of the Gospel, at 2.13–22. It is one of the very first things Jesus does. And John also stresses that Jesus is arrested and put to death at the time when Jerusalem is packed with pilgrims come for the festival of the Passover. He dies at precisely the same time as the Passover lambs are being slaughtered in the temple. For the Roman authorities, never mind those Jews who hold power in the temple, this is a most sensitive time, when any disturbance can easily get out of hand and escalate into a full-blown riot, if not a larger rebellion. Things must be nipped in the bud. So Jesus is quickly executed. But for the authorities that cannot be the end of it. They must remain extremely vigilant, to make sure this man's followers do not start to make trouble, and this could well mean they must go looking for them. The disciples certainly have plenty to fear, both from Pilate and his troops and the Jewish temple police.

And into this gathering, where there is such fear, but where there is also the fearless Mary of Magdala with her extraordinary news, Jesus comes with his twice-repeated, 'Peace be with you.' It is a version of that 'Do not be afraid', which in the Bible is so often God's way of introducing himself. They are the same words as Jesus uses in Luke 24.36, when he first appears to all the disciples together.

The greeting is designed to do more than offer reassurance. It is meant to give courage and energy for the task ahead. It is meant to spur them into getting up, unlocking the doors, and going out into the streets of Jerusalem and beyond. 'As the Father sent me, so I send you.' Their task is the same one that Jesus has had: it is God's task. If they remain behind their locked doors, the resurrection will mean nothing. As John Dominic Crossan puts it, the resurrection is less about the exaltation of Christ, and more about the transformation of the world, about collaborating with 'the non-violent God of justice and peace' that Jesus has shown us, proclaiming and promoting 'God's Great Clean-Up of the earth', the 'taking back of God's world from the thugs' (*The Resurrection of Jesus: The Crossan–Wright Dialogue*, pp. 179, 181, 186). Paul knew that well, of course, and he knew equally well how dangerous that work could be. It had taken Jesus to the cross. It took Paul to imprisonments, floggings, a stoning, to the very edge of death on several occasions (see 2 Corinthians 11.23–29). John himself will finish his Gospel by speaking of the martyrdom that will one day face Peter, and in the passage we are exploring, at the moment when he turns disciples into apostles and sends them out, Jesus stands before them with hands pierced by cruel nails and the gash of a soldier's spear in his side.

So the disciples are sent out to carry Jesus' vision, Jesus' practice, Jesus' ways of being and doing out into the world. In the other three Gospels this sending out is anticipated when Jesus sends out the Twelve to teach and heal (Mark 6.3–13; Matthew 10.5–15; Luke 9.1–6), and in Luke 10.1–12 there is the further story of Jesus sending 70 or 72 of his disciples ahead of him as he begins his journey to Jerusalem. John waits till the day of resurrection.

In Matthew, Jesus promises his disciples that he will always be with them. In Luke he assures them that they will be 'clothed with power from on high'. But Luke keeps that moment of empowerment in reserve. He does not speak of it in his Gospel, but instead in the second chapter of Acts, when the Holy Spirit descends on the disciples with the sound of a roaring wind and the strange sight of tongues of flame (2.1–4). The Church has again allowed Luke to determine its liturgical calendar, marking Pentecost, as well as the ascension, according to his chronology. If it had followed John instead, it would have celebrated the gift of the Holy Spirit on the evening of Easter Day.

The gift is given more quietly in John. No wind, no tongues of flame, but instead, 'breath'. It is a more intimate moment than in Luke, for it is the breath of the risen Jesus. He is there in their midst, whereas in Luke he has already been taken from them into heaven. And 'breathing on them' brings him very close, as close as it brings God in the Garden of Eden, when he breathes the life into the first human being (Genesis 2.7). There he shapes the creature from the dust, and breathes the life into it through its nostrils, so that it becomes a living being. In my mind's eye I see God bending low over his creature and putting his mouth over its nose. Because the writer of the story knows exactly how far to go in using human language of God, he does not talk in those terms, but leaves ample room for the mystery of the divine. Yet there is no doubt that his verse is an expression of astonishing intimacy, of what I call 'the intimacy with which we were made, the intimacy for which we were made' (my book *Looking God in the Eye*, 1998, p. 5).

That same ancient intimacy of God is here inside the locked room. The recalling of Genesis 2.7 is surely deliberate. John means us to see this act of empowerment as a new act of creation. He began his Gospel with those solemn, momentous words:

> In the beginning was the Word,
> and the Word was with God,
> and the Word was God.
> He was in the beginning with God.
> All things came to be through him,
> And without him nothing came into being . . .
> And the Word became flesh and pitched his tent
>   among us.
>
> (John 1.1–3, 14a)

Those words took us back to the beginnings of creation, when the one who 'became flesh', who came to speak with the accent of a Galilean Jew, was 'with God', and 'was God'. The resurrection has at last made sense of those lines. Jesus is in the midst of his disciples as their Lord and their God, as Thomas soon will testify. He is there as their Creator, they are once more in Eden, so what more appropriate than that he should breathe upon them and fill them with new energy, new life, new courage for the task of showing the world what it means to be human?

He sends them out trailing both forgiveness and judgement. John has made clear throughout his Gospel that in Jesus the world finds itself judged and, indeed, condemned. That is a way of emphasizing just how radical Jesus' vision is, and how very hard it is for people to put into practice. For it does not simply demand that individuals change their ambitions and their lifestyles. It requires that society and the relations between societies be structured in entirely new ways. It requires, for example, that violence should not be met with violence, but with the washing of tired and bloody feet.

John's talk in John 20.23, however, about the forgiving or 'holding' of sins is somewhat unnerving. The language of 'holding' sins is somewhat obscure (which is why we have offered such a literal translation). There is a verse in Matthew, twice repeated, where Jesus gives Peter 'the keys of heaven' and declares, 'Whatever you bind on earth will be bound in heaven, and whatever you loose on earth will be loosed in heaven' (Matthew 16.19; 18.18). Some suggest that Matthew is here asserting Peter's authority to decide which of the Jewish laws are binding for the members of the Church, and which can be annulled (see Warren Carter, *Matthew and the Margins*, p. 336). But John cannot mean that here in 20.23, for he is talking specifically of the forgiveness of sins, or the refusal to forgive them.

It is unnerving talk, because it seems to place such frightening authority into the hands of human beings, authority that we will almost certainly misuse, and that indeed we already have. And more seriously still, it seems to set limits on what is after all not our forgiveness, but God's. The Parable of the Father and the Two Lost Sons, with its images of the father running helter-skelter up the road to greet one of his sons, and dropping that quiet word *teknon* into the rage of the other, gives us a picture of a God whose forgiveness refuses any limits, but is all-embracing, a God whose forgiveness is our starting point, our middle and our end.

But there is still one passage in John to consider, and that will bring the parable back to mind and reinforce its vision.

'Feed my sheep'

The final passage we shall consider follows on from the 'Come and have breakfast' story in John 21. It does not, in fact, re-present John's last words, for he has a short passage on the beloved disciple and the rumour flying around in his community that he would not die, and after that two verses that bring the work formally (once again) to an end. We need not concern ourselves with those, but only with 21.15–19:

> When they had finished breakfast, Jesus said to Simon Peter, 'Simon son of John, do you love me more than these?' He replied, 'Yes, Lord. You know I love you.' Jesus said to him, 'Feed my lambs.' A second time he asked him, 'Simon son of John, do you love me?' He replied, 'Yes, Lord. You know I love you.' He said to him, 'Tend my sheep.' A third time he asked him, 'Simon son of John, do you love me?' Peter was grieved that he asked him for the third time, 'Do you love me?' He replied, 'Lord, you know everything; you know I love you.' Jesus said to him, 'Feed my sheep. Truly, truly I tell you, when you were younger, you fastened your own belt to go wherever you wished. But when you grow old, then you will stretch out your hands, and another will fasten a belt around you, and you will go where you do not wish to go.' (He said this to indicate the kind of death by which he would glorify God.) Then he said to him, 'Follow me.'

With just these verses in front of us, we would picture the seven disciples still sitting round the charcoal fire with Jesus. But the next verse, 21.20, begins, 'Peter turned round and

117

noticed the disciple whom Jesus loved following them.' So instead, we must imagine that Jesus has taken Peter away from the others, and is walking with him along the shore, while the beloved disciple follows behind.

Applying the terms of contemporary psychology to the characterization of Peter in these scenes, Mark Stibbe suggests we see him as being in denial. 'Having failed Jesus so obviously in 18.15–27,' he writes (the reference is to the passage about Peter's denial),

> he now seeks to suppress and even obliterate the shame in his life by reverting to 'life before Christ', to fishing. He seeks to deny the three denials. This attempt to fill his 'hole in the soul' with work fails dismally. The narrator laconically remarks that 'they caught nothing.'
>
> (*John*, p. 210)

We have already noticed the significance of the charcoal fire and the timing of the dawn. The references back to Peter's denial are unmistakable. On that same page of his commentary Stibbe points out another detail of John's story of Peter's denial, or rather a detail that it lacks. In Mark 14.72, Matthew 26.75 and Luke 22.62, at the end of their versions of the story of the denial, Peter breaks down and weeps. In Matthew and Luke he weeps 'bitterly'. All those who know J. S. Bach's *St Matthew Passion* will recall how the narrator sings those words, 'and he went outside and wept bitterly'. It is one of the most poignant and powerful moments in the whole work. But it is not there in his *St John Passion*, for the simple reason that John's text contains no reference to Peter's tears. His passage concludes with the words, 'Again Peter denied it, and immediately a cock crowed.' John does not allow Peter there to express his grief, or his sense of shame and failure. Instead, he must bottle them up, suppress them, and end up going fishing to try to forget them.

So one purpose of Jesus' questioning him is to allow that grief to be faced. It works. By the time Jesus asks his question for a third time, Peter is 'grieved' ('hurt', which many translations give, is too weak; the Greek term is derived from the word for grief). The facing of shame and failure such as Peter's is always painful, and Jesus does not spare him the pain. Not only does he ask him the question three times, to match his threefold denial, but he calls him 'Simon son of John'. That is what he calls him the very first time he meets him: 'You are Simon son of John' (John 1.42). Such formal address takes them both right back to the beginning. They must start again. Peter must not simply return to that terrible moment of denial, but must work his mind through everything they have been through together. Three times he has denied he was ever a disciple of Jesus. Now, for the relationship to be restored, he must be taken right back to the point when first he encountered Jesus, and must hear those life-changing words, 'Follow me.'

Jesus' questioning works for another reason, a deeper reason still: the breakfast has already taken place. Peter has already heard that invitation, 'Come and have breakfast.' It has not been a feast for him with fatted calf and music and dancing. It has been the simple meal of fish and bread of the peasant God. But it has been as good as any feast the Roman emperor could provide, and much finer. John does not have the Parable of the Father and the Two Lost Sons in his Gospel, but he makes no mistake here: he puts forgiveness and acceptance first, and then Peter's repentance. And precisely because forgiveness is already in place, Peter can come to a full repentance. Grief is faced, shame is acknowledged, threefold denial is answered with threefold protestation of love. If he had been met with Jesus' condemnation, he would have crumpled, and would not have been able to move on. He would have jumped from his boat and sunk down beyond rescue in guilt and despair.

Jesus accepts his declarations of love with full seriousness. He does not simply say to Peter, 'That is what I wanted to hear.' He gives him a job to do. Three times he gives it to him, the job of looking after his sheep. Back in John 10, Peter has heard him speak of the 'good shepherd' who cares for the sheep and is prepared if necessary to die for them. Jesus there contrasts that shepherd with the hired hand, who when he sees a wolf coming, runs away. Peter has behaved like a hired hand, but now Jesus appoints him to the role he has himself played, that of the shepherd. It has cost Jesus. It will cost Peter. He too will stretch his hands out on a cross, and be taken to a cruel death he does not want. But he will die the shepherd. He will not run away again. His days as a hired hand are over.

5

Reflections

————◆•◆————

I study, sometimes teach, and occasionally write about the
Bible. As a priest working in a cathedral I also find myself regu-
larly preaching on it, and as Easter Day and the Easter season
come round every year, I am faced with the task of saying
something fresh, that enables us to connect with the resurrection stories and get a little deeper into them. It is not easy!
Sometimes I use poetry or storytelling, offering the whole sermon as a poem or story, for that is the only way I can begin
to express what I wish to say. I discovered that way of preaching (at least storytelling) when I was a school chaplain in the
1970s and, after a break of a few years, I continued with it
when I taught in a theological college, and again when I came
to Chester Cathedral in 1994, since when more of my pieces
have emerged in poetic form. SPCK has published five collections of those pieces over the years. We will bring this present volume to an end with seven pieces, all written since I
have been at Chester. 'The walk to Emmaus' was published in
The Three Faces of Christ (1999), and 'Ascension Day' and
'Peter's story' in *Keeping God Company* (2002). The first three
pieces and the last have not been published before.

In entering into the stories of resurrection from the
Gospels, we crossed that shining line and stepped into the
circle of the divine. We found ourselves in a strange and
wonderful world, where large stones at the doors of tombs are
swept away like dead leaves; where death does not hold sway
any more, its tight, dark places empty but for the rustling
sound of angels' wings; where the acknowledged centres of
power no longer count; where, wonder of wonders, we meet
a wounded God marked with the scars of crucifixion; where
those who have denied and deserted take their place once

more in the circle and sit and eat; where, against all reasonable expectation, there is good news to be told and hopes are renewed and fulfilled, and new ones, undreamed of, are born; where a task is given, that of collaborating with the wounded God to establish his topsy-turvy kingdom on this, his bright earth; where the ancient intimacy of God is recovered, and through it the energy and the courage for that great task. The following reflections represent attempts to grapple with the reality of that world.

In none of them have I kept strictly to any particular version of a resurrection story in the Gospels. I have brought my own imagination to bear, played with the text, and sometimes laid one text upon another. That is part of the freedom that storytelling or poetry gives, and one of the reasons I sometimes choose those forms for preaching. My play is never, I hope, casual or disrespectful. I am not indulging in clever games here, but simply trying to preach the Gospel as powerfully as I can.

Transfiguration

Finding God at the top of a mountain
is not so very surprising.
Mountains are bigger than we are.
They put things into perspective,
lift us above the humdrum,
remove us from what is routine.
Mountains are never trivial.
They take our breath away.

Peoples have said for millennia
their gods have lived on mountains.
They have talked much sense.
When mountains have not been available
for holy eyes to look upon,
then some have built them for themselves,
great ziggurats puncturing their flat horizons,
to ensure their gods are close,
but not too intimate.

Finding God at the top of a mountain
is not so very surprising.

Had not Moses once met God on Sinai's jagged rock?
Had not God called to him
from a cloud bright with divinity?
Had not God talked to him face to face,
as one speaks to a friend,
sharing his secrets with him,
making him his confidant,
causing his face to shine with such a light,
that he dazzled them all
when he walked into the camp,
knowing nothing of it,
until he saw them shielding their eyes,
turning their faces away?
(His face blazed with the light of heaven,
and he did not know it.
How's that for humility?)

And had not Elijah fled to the same mountain,
run home for God's mothering
against the deadly Jezebel?
And had not God spoken with him there,
even though the carnival of wind and quake and fire
was that time but an empty show?

Finding God on a mountain
is not so very surprising,
though once, they say,
the devil took Jesus to the top of one,
to show him all the kingdoms of the world,
to make their people seem so very small
and easy for his taking.
But then the devil never did understand mountains;
they never took *his* breath away.

What was surprising
was the God we found up there,
for we had heard him many times before,
we knew his tones of voice,

the looks in his eye,
the limp in his gait
(as though he had wrestled with an angel
through long hours of the night).
He was our fellow-traveller,
our master and our slave,
father to us, mother, too,
healer, teacher, brother, friend.
We knew where he came from,
and it was no heavenly city
of jasper, gold and clear as glass,
but Nazareth, a nowhere place.
We knew where he was going:
Jerusalem, to torture and to death.
You cannot have God killed, for God's sake!

And yet there, up there,
on the top of the mountain
we walked straight into God
and recognized him,
for the first time.

He made the strange familiar
and the familiar strange.
His face put the sun in the shade
and his clothes made the wheeling storks look dull.
The rock of the summit,
shaved bare by frost and wind,
was carpeted with flowers,
while far above our heads the eagles gathered for the
    dance.
The mountain leopard lost her shyness,
came out from her hiding,
rolled on her back at his feet
ready to lie down with the kid.
The very air held its breath.

And we?
We did not know what to do with ourselves,
but thought of that ancient tent of meeting,

and supposed one, or three, would be appropriate,
marking a place where heaven touched the earth
and could be found again,
a holy mountain bothy,
built of rams' skins,
enough to hold out against the cold and wind.

It was not such a foolish idea,
but this, our new-found God,
was for moving on to another mountain,
the one we call Mount Zion
(too full, as it turned out, of its own importance,
and far too grand a place for the pitching of tents).
Our God would not have us traipsing up our
    mountain,
this mountain of transfiguration,
to bend aside the tent-flaps
and speak with him from time to time.
Our God wanted our companionship on his journey to
    Jerusalem.

And so we gave it to him.
We kept him company.
To Gethsemane, at least,
where we left him to a lonely, abandoned Golgotha.

We had wondered,
when we found him on the mountain,
why his hands and feet were pierced.

How can you meet an angel?

How can you meet an angel?
Is it like bumping into the woman next door,
while you're carrying water back from the well,
and you say, 'Hello Sarah,
missed you at the well today;
are you all right?
Is your back too sore?
Are the children not able to carry for you?

Are they sick with a fever again?
And how's your Nathan?
Did he get any work at the vineyard,
or was he hanging around at the market place all day,
with nothing for you to cook at the end of it?'
Is that how it is when you meet an angel,
so you go back to the well the next day
and say to your friends,
'Guess what. Met an angel yesterday.
Nice angel he was
(or was it a she?)
can't really say with angels, can you?
My Rachel's come out in spots, by the way.'

Is that how it is when you meet an angel?
'Of course it isn't!
Angels lift you off your feet, they do,
give you wings, they do,
take you to another world
that smells and tastes of heaven,
and when you come back down to earth,
it's like seeing it for the first time,
and then you understand.

So when we found an angel in his tomb,
it was, you might say, unnerving.
The last place to find an angel, surely,
sitting in a cupboard made for death.

We'd been at Golgotha.
No angels there.
None that we saw, anyway.
Soldiers, yes;
gawpers, plenty;
scoffers? Them too.
No angels, though,
just when we needed them,
or he did, poor love,
our friend,
companion on the road,

teacher,
footwasher,
cook and bottle washer,
the one who introduced us to God.
Those bandits beside him
could have done with an angel or two, as well,
to lift them out of their agony.
I don't know what they'd done,
but they didn't deserve that.
No one deserves a death like theirs,
like his.
But the angels didn't come,
and the band didn't play 'When the saints come
    marching in',
and we didn't dance or roll our hips
or turn our heads and laugh.
There was no miracle, see.
Least, there *was*,
but we couldn't see very well at the time, or hear.
Crucifixion's a noisy business.

It was quieter by the tomb,
though we still couldn't see for grief.
We'd come for women's work,
although another woman had seen to it already,
in Simon the leper's house at Bethany.
Smothered him in ointment, she had.
Done it properly,
no messing;
well a lot of mess,
but holy mess,
beautiful mess,
ponging to high heaven.
But by the time Pilate had finished with him
and his brave soldier men,
he didn't smell so good any more,
so we came to do it again,
with our spices from the market,
and the know-how in our hands.

We'd laid out children and husbands between us,
as well as friends and neighbours.
We knew what to do.

That was, until we met the angel.
Took the stuffing right out of us, it did.
Didn't see him, exactly.
Well, you can't, can you?
But you know one's there, when he's there,
or she. He, she, it, there's no word for an angel.

The angel gave us wings,
feet off the ground,
to another world,
took us to meet him,
our friend, the footwasher,
not in the tomb,
oh, no, not there,
not in death's cupboard,
but on a high mountain apart,
in our familiar Galilee,
and there he was,
coming to meet us,
with his clothes all dazzling white,
as even Rachel couldn't bleach them
(and Rachel's good at bleaching, is Rachel),
and he put his arms around us,
and kissed us again and again,
like we were his children,
and he'd been waiting for us a long time
and we'd just come from a land far away.
He dressed us up for a village wedding,
our wedding, as if we were young again,
and sat us down to fatted calf,
'But first I'll wash your feet,' he said.

And then we saw his hands, of course,
noticed his feet and the gash in his side.
Our ointments came in handy, after all.

When we came back to earth,
it was like seeing it for the first time,
and now we understand.

Teaching God to dance

All that Luke says about Mary of Magdala, when we first hear of her in 8.2, is that Jesus had healed her from 'seven demons'. Such language indicates that her condition was extremely severe and considered incurable. It need not have been what we would now call mental illness, though it could do, and I have made it so. There is no suggestion in Luke, or any of the other Gospels, that Mary was the victim of domestic violence, as I describe her in this piece. The issues of such abuse are at last being brought out into the open, and some in Chester Diocese, with strong support from the bishop, have been tackling them with energy and vision for some years now. Perhaps that helps to explain why, when I sat down to write a story-sermon for the Cathedral for Easter Day 2006, I found myself using my imagination in the way I did.

When I was a girl in Magdala my mother told me ancient stories of God and my people, the Jews. One began like this: 'And it happened after these things that God tested Abraham. And he said to him, "Abraham!" and he said, "Here I am." And he said, "Take, pray, your son, your only one, whom you love, Isaac . . . and offer him up as a burnt offering . . ."'

I hated that story. I thought its God was a monster. 'What about Sarah?' I asked my mother. 'Did God ask her to go as well?'

'No,' my mother replied.

'Why not?'

'Because . . . You will learn why in due time, Mary.'

'You mean it was because she was a woman and women don't count.'

'You are too old for your years, Mary,' my mother said.

Another night she told me the story of Moses and the burning bush. 'Only a bush?' I said. 'Not a great tree? I thought

gods had sacred trees, not bushes. Does that mean our God
was not big enough to have a tree, only a stupid bush?'

My mother looked at me. 'Only the God of all the universe
would be content with a bush,' she replied.

I may have been too old for my years, but I didn't understand that.

'And God called to him,' she continued, 'from the midst of
the bush and said, "Moses, Moses!" And he said, "Here I am."
Then he said, "Come no closer here. Take off your sandals
from your feet, for the place you are standing on is holy
ground."'

'But Moses was married to Zipporah at the time,' I inter-
rupted. 'Tell me a story about God saying to Zipporah,
"Zipporah, Zipporah!"'

'There isn't one,' my mother said.

'Might've guessed,' I said.

When it came to the story of the boy Samuel, and God
waking him in the night over and over with his 'Samuel,
Samuel!' I'd had enough. 'I don't want to know,' I said.

When I grew up and started my periods and got married
to a rich man with lots of slaves and animals and barns
not big enough for his harvests, I learned afresh that women
didn't count. He hit me on our wedding night. He hit me
every night. And every night he raped me. There's no other
word for it. And when, to my despair, I found myself preg-
nant with his child and couldn't hide it from him any more,
he shouted, 'Why didn't you tell me? Are you ashamed of it?
It's a girl, is it? Is that it? A filth of a girl curled up inside you!
Well, we'll see about that!' And he kicked me in the stomach
and kept kicking me until he'd finished and the child inside
me was dead. He divorced me after that. Because I couldn't
have children any more and was incapable of giving him a
son.

And that is why, when Jesus came to Magdala, he found me
mad. My family were ashamed of me and had shut me in a
small, windowless room, never allowing me out. They even
gave up using my name. I crouched in the corner of that
room, swaying back and forth. Or else I danced, a slow, awk-
ward, gangly dance, that got faster and faster, until I would

fall on the floor, exhausted. Jesus of Nazareth found me in that room. I was dancing. 'Don't touch me!' I shouted. He waited and waited, waited till I fell in a heap at his feet. 'Mary!' he said. And then, after a long pause, and very quietly, 'Follow me.'

And so I did, of course. From village to village, to city, to grand temple, to crucifixion, to death, to burial.

Then there was nothing I could do for him any more. Except dance. That is why I went to the tomb, to dance for him outside. He wouldn't be able to see, of course. The stone would be between us, and in any case he was dead. But I would dance and dance and dance, until I fell exhausted to the ground, and then I would hope for death to come to me, too, so we could be together, him and me.

But he wasn't in the tomb. It was full of angels, instead. No room for him. I was in a different world. Somewhere along the path through the garden I'd crossed the line between earth and heaven, between the empire of Augustus and the kingdom of God. But I hadn't seen it. It was still dark, I suppose, though that seems a feeble excuse. I was blind with grief. That's a better one, I guess. In this new world of God, dead bodies were replaced by angels. Only I didn't want angels. I wanted him.

'They've taken him away!' I cried. I didn't know who 'they' were, but they must have put him somewhere and I wanted to find out, so I could go and pick him up and hold him in my arms, as once, in that small, dark, fetid room in Magdala, he had held me till my madness had gone and I had found my sanity. 'Mary!' he had said. Now I would hold him and call his name over and over, and it would do no good, but I'd be able to say there was nothing more I could have done and try one day to kid myself out of grief.

But he wasn't there. At some point I'd crossed over into the kingdom of God, but I didn't know it. I had met angels, for God's sake, but still I didn't realize where I was! I thought I was in the world where people could take bodies out of tombs too posh for them and dump them on the rubbish heap, and where men beat their wives and kicked the foetuses out of them. I didn't really notice the angels. At least, I did, but it didn't sink in. I panicked, you see. All I wanted was him, to dance for him, to hold him, for one last time.

Something made me turn round. I thought he was the gardener. I asked him whether he had taken Jesus away. Why in heaven's name would a gardener do such a thing? I wasn't thinking straight. Grief's like that, of course. You think silly things and sometimes you say them out loud.

'Mary!' he said.

'Here I am,' I replied.

I went to embrace him, to hold him, as once he had held me. But you can't get your arms round God. So I took off my sandals for the dance instead. I held out my hands to him.

'I cannot dance,' he said. 'The nails,' he said. 'You have a limping God, now, Mary.'

'Then I will teach you a limping dance,' I replied. 'Once you were my teacher. You taught me how to dance. Not that jagged, exhausting dance of my madness and my rage, but the dance of your very particular kind of sanity, "The Dance of the Kingdom of God" you called it. Now I will be your teacher, and after we have done, then I will wash your feet. You taught me how to do that, too.'

And that is how I taught my God to dance.

The walk to Emmaus

He began as a stranger,
one who happened to be going in the same direction,
a pilgrim, they presumed,
returning from Jerusalem,
from a Passover lost in grief and overtaken by death.
He began as one they thought must live in a world of
    his own,
cut off in empty loneliness,
or else plain stupid.
He became on the way their companion,
their teacher,
at home their guest,
their host and hostess

(for *he* took bread and blessed and broke and gave it),
and finally,
with eyes opened,
their God.

Have you ever heard of such a thing?
Yes, once in Eden,
in the garden he planted,
near the place where grew a tree weighed down with
    knowledge,
and another with enough life to overcome death,
at the centre of the garden
God came walking,
and the hearts of the man and woman burned within
    them,
and they too came to know their foolishness.
Each of them had known God's intimacy
at their creation,
God's hands upon them,
God's breath on their faces,
God's warm, passionate kiss of life.
Later, near the Tree of Knowledge,
near the neglected Tree of Life,
they knew his intimacy again,
as he came walking in the cool of the day,
with footsteps they could hear upon the garden's gravel
    paths.
But that story ended differently,
not with recognition,
for they knew him already and were afraid,
not with him bending low
to come inside their tent, as at Mamre,
not with him sitting cross-legged beside their fire,
nor with the breaking of bread, as at Emmaus,
nor with blessing, the surprise of joy,
but with expulsion and estrangement.
We speak of a loss of innocence in Eden,
and so there was.

Yet there was a larger loss of intimacy,
the intimacy of those acts of creation,
the intimacy we were made for.

On the road to Emmaus,
in a small house,
in a smaller room,
at a meal,
that ancient intimacy was found again.
We call that rediscovery
'resurrection'.

Some of it was played out long before,
beneath the oaks of Mamre,
where Abraham snoozed and Sarah worked,
when God came out of the heat of the sun,
without announcement,
without ceremony
(beyond the usual hospitalities),
and sat and ate.
That was a return to the old intimacy,
the one for which we all were made.
It was a moving on, also,
to hope beyond imagining,
and grief was turned to joy.
For there was new birth,
a new life beyond all expectation
(for Isaac was born when Sarah was ninety years of
    age,
and Abraham one hundred,
or so the story goes –
stories of resurrection are like that).
Yet there was no moment of recognition.
Even at the story's end
Abraham did not know his guest's identity.
Though the stranger knew his wife's name
without any telling,
promised a child,
without hesitation,
gave the date of birth,

heard Sarah's silent laugh,
Abraham never tumbled to him,
never said, 'My Lord and my God!'
never went running to his friends,
never spoke of resurrection.
Maybe Sarah realized,
but the oaks of Mamre do not tell us so.
Their story remains unfinished,
waiting an ending.

At Emmaus,
in a smoky room,
over a meal,
at the breaking of some bread,
at a moment of eternal simplicity,
when the guest became,
without rudeness or presumption,
the host
and hostess, too,
then it found, that ancient story,
a proper conclusion.
Emmaus was made into Eden,
the flaming sword blocking all entrance
revealed as a figment of our guilt and fear-filled
    imagination.
The old intimacy was recovered,
seen and felt for what it was,
and this time shared in resurrection.

What ending does our story come to now?
Might we feel God's hands upon us,
God's breath upon our faces,
God's kiss?
Might we find hope beyond imagining
and grief turned all to joy,
new birth,
new life beyond all expectation?
Might we tumble to it all,
and know that we have stumbled upon resurrection?

I cannot answer that.
But I can assure you
God tried to teach Abraham and Sarah
to prepare for surprises.

Ascension Day

'What can this mean,
this ascension?
Is it cause for celebration,
or for grief?
Is it triumph,
or parting?
So much hangs on the answer.
The stories tell of both.
They speak of parting,
disappearance,
of Christ going away
to where we cannot follow –
not till death brings
our own resurrection and ascension.
Yet they also speak of triumph,
of glory,
exaltation,
heaven all a-ring with alleluias.
Which of these is of the truth?'

'Both of them, my friend.
The stories can be trusted.
Ascension is both triumph and parting,
two faces of the same,
a time for sorrow and a time for joy.
We speak of the cross
as the place of Christ's triumph,
and so it was.
But triumph then
was not without its fearsome ambiguity.
How can we call such brutality
as was there on Golgotha,

such pain and fighting for breath,
such inevitable dying,
such utter loneliness,
where even God himself
seemed to hide for very fear,
how can we call that triumph,
and say no more?
It was, of course, a victory
for reconciliation,
for generosity,
for humility,
for integrity,
for courage,
for love,
for meekness strong as steel,
for all that is good.
Of course it was.
Resurrection taught us that,
and ring out alleluias for it!
But we cannot leave it there.
We cannot leave God there.

'Let Christ be put aloft
in heavenly double-decker bus!
Let him be paraded
through the streets of the heavenly Jerusalem,
holding up the cross for all to see!
Let him be deafened
by the cheers of angels!
Let God be reunited,
instead of torn to pieces!
Let Christ feel the warmth again
of the divine embrace!
For God's sake let him know
God had not deserted him!
Let him get the mockery of the soldiers
and the fears of the priests
out of his head!
Let him know love,

let him be fair bathed in it!
Let him drink the wine of heaven,
instead of the vinegar of Golgotha!
Let him take his place once more
in the dance and the laughter
of the Trinity!
Oh yes,
let that be,
let that be!

'And let us catch the echoes
of all this celebrating,
and have a chance
to throw our own caps in the air!

'Let all manner of things,
all manner of things be well,
and let us know,
deep in the depths of our souls,
that that is so.
Let us glimpse,
behind the ambiguity
of this familiar world,
another realm,
where God is love,
and God is loved,
and that is all there is.
No caveats,
no qualifications,
no yes buts.
God is love,
God is loved,
and that is all there is.

'This familiar world of ours
is too full of caveats,
and qualifications,
of yes buts,
and worse.
Even on heady days,

when hope runs high,
we know it will not last.
God will be denied again;
we will deny God again,
and fail once more
to come to terms with an eternal love
that is so utterly unencumbered with strings,
and given with such wild, unstinting prodigality.
All is not well here,
nor, while we are around,
will ever be.

'God is absent here,
as much as God is present,
or that is how it feels.
For us it is one
of the world's enduring realities.
We face it every day.

'Preachers will tell you
that Ascension Day
is not about Christ's going away
and leaving us behind.
Yet that is how the ancient story goes,
and those the terms in which it speaks.
And for us,
in this place,
it is part of the truth of it,
part of our truth,
and part of God's, also.
God does not belong here,
though he made his home here,
long before Bethlehem,
long before the earth was marked
by any human print.
God does not belong here,
because we have shut the door on him.
It is as simple as that,
and as devastating.

'So God belongs in heaven,
and must return there,
while we are left behind,
for the moment,
till our own resurrection and ascension,
till our own reunion,
with ourselves,
with one another,
with creation,
with God.
Till that moment comes
we are left behind
to do God's work,
give him some cooperation,
hang out the bunting,
put up the balloons,
put on the kettle,
and bid him welcome.

'For, of course, God does belong here, too.
This is God's home,
as much as heaven.
He has been here
before we were a twinkle in his eye,
This is God's home,
this *is* God's home,
and we must set about as best we can,
and make him welcome.'

Peter's story

Storytelling provides an opportunity to mix the contemporary with the old. So into the story of Peter beside the Sea of Galilee I have woven some of my own memories of visiting that lake with various groups of pilgrims, and of joining in celebrations of the Eucharist on its shores.

It was early. The sun was still hidden behind the Golan hills, the churches of the holy sites were not yet open, and the buses full of pilgrims were not yet on the road. The Sea of Galilee – or the Sea of Kingfishers as I call it, there are so many of them there – lay very quiet. Only the smallest of waves ruffled the shoreline. White egrets flew silently from their roosts, and the first kingfishers began diving for their fish, disturbing the dawn with small splashes, emerging with little fish shining in their bills. The air shone with unusual clarity. In the far distance the high snows of Mount Hermon turned pink in the new sun.

We'd gone back to our fishing. We were trying to forget. Turn the clock back and go back to the beginning. Go back to Galilee, to familiar waters, to the old boats and the old ways. As if nothing had occurred. Push out the boats, cast the nets, haul them in, as if nothing had happened.

But, of course, it had. There was no pretending. You cannot go back to the beginning, because when you get there you find it has changed from when you started out. You cannot undo the past. You cannot go back to a past you would prefer to remember, as if the in-between, the things you long to forget, had never been. Escape is not that easy, nor that possible.

Of course, there were things in-between we wanted to remember. Jesus himself for one, and his jokes, and the parties we had into the small hours, and his strange, disturbing stories and the words he came out with, and his uncanny knack of reaching the heart of everyone he met, and the way he turned things upside down, and his getting so angry with those who thought religion was more important than people, and the friendships he created. All that we wanted to remember. But not the journey to Jerusalem and the soldiers. Not the pleading with him to be more careful. Not the telling him to stop being so stupid. Not the, who did he think he was, the bloody Messiah? and him reminding me that that was precisely what I'd said he was just a moment before. I didn't want to remember that. Nor Herod and Pilate. Nor the pretence of a trial, and the sham of another, and his yells as he was being beaten. Nor the courtyard of the high priest's house and the charcoal fire. I didn't want to remember that. God! I didn't want to remember that.

Yet I kept on remembering. Over and over again. How cold it was that night of the trial. How glad I was of the fire. How I was sitting there all in a daze, thinking I was safe, when that wretched slave-girl recognized me. 'Hey, you were with him!' she shouted. She said it again later. Told everyone she did. Then the others heard my northern accent and started joining in, and before I knew it, the dawn came and the cock crowed.

I got the hell out of it. I missed the crucifixion. So did the others. Except Mary of Magdala and the other women. They'd always had a rare courage, ever since he'd cured them of their terrible illnesses. After that they'd never cared about anyone else. The soldiers would have had to kill them to keep them away.

But I wasn't there. I'd done a runner. I'd failed. I'd let him down. Three times I'd said I didn't even know who he was. And I wasn't there when he died. I'd funked it. I'd gone away to hide in a corner. Mary and her friends had been made of sterner stuff, and had a deeper love for him than I did. When it came to it I didn't love him enough. It was as simple as that.

So there we were, out fishing on the Sea of Galilee, pretending we were back where we began. We were fools! For God's sake, we were back where it had all started with *him*! The place was full of him. You could smell him in the air. His voice was in the cries of the birds. The shore was marked all over by his steps. Even the waters of the lake seemed to have his stamp upon them. And this time there was no escape, no doing a runner, no hiding in a corner.

Another charcoal fire was burning on the shore, like the one in the courtyard of the high priest's house. 'Come and have breakfast,' he called. In a few hours' time the busloads of pilgrims would be scattering themselves beside the shore, huddling round their bread and wine. We were there already, with his bread and our fish.

Three times he asked me if I loved him. Three times he gave me the chance to replace denial with love. Three times I took that chance. And three times he called me shepherd of his sheep. Do you know what shepherd means? Long before David and Solomon, long before our ancestors came to this land, kings called themselves 'shepherds' of their people. Jesus was calling me king, and that breakfast of bread and fish was my coronation banquet! But what sort of king should I be? I didn't have to ask that. I just had to remember how he had exercised his royalty, with a towel round his waist, and at the last, when they'd got round to his enthronement, a cross for a throne.

I've hurt him more times than three since then. I'm only human, after all, not the saint of your stained-glass windows. But I've found the love for him that Mary of Magdala and the other women always had, and the strength and the courage that goes with it. How could I not love him, when he took the script of my denial and burned it to ashes in a charcoal fire, and filled the air of Galilee with talk of love, and then placed a crown on my head? 'You look ridiculous!' he cried then, and our laughter was so loud, a group of early pilgrims turned in our direction and scowled at us for disturbing their devotions. 'But then,' he added more quietly, 'I too looked ridiculous on that cross, me, the king of the Jews, and the very Son of God. Wear your crown with courage, my old friend. And remember, the love is mutual.'

I have not forgotten.

The fire of God's hospitality

This very short piece owes a very great deal to the psalms, especially Psalm 84. Yet it is also a commentary on the resurrection, and in particular on John's story of the breakfast beside the Sea of Galilee and the dialogue with Peter.

How beautiful the place where you dwell, O God!
You fill it to bursting with your delight!
Here is the beating of your heart;
here the air carries your scent,
and the soft tread of your footfall.
Here you have the freedom to play,
and we the knowledge we are loved.

We long for this with all our heart and soul,
long to know we count for something and always will,

long to know our names are written on the palm of
  your hand,
that we are the apple of your eye, and always will be,
no matter what,
no matter what.

This is holy ground;
where we can take off the shoes of our fear.
Here we are known,
understood, embraced, forgiven.
Here is a coming together,
a mingling of heaven and earth,
and the making of community.

This is holy ground,
and we are safe.
Even the birds find a home here,
the raven a nest where she may lay her young.
The place where you dwell, O God,
is our home also.
We have crossed your threshold,
and know we have come home.
Here the barriers between us
crumble to dust and blow away.

This is common ground.
Here is God's welcome;
here burns the fire of God's hospitality.
None are turned away here.
For here is the generosity of heaven
and the community of creation.

Let us then care for one another.
Let us care for God's world,
And join with him in its remaking.